I0418400

# For the Record:

# The Testimonies of Mary Magdalene
# and
# Judas Iscariot

*Second Edition*

Cynthia Farrar Burse

The testimonies given by Mary Magdalene and Judas Iscariot are products of the author's imagination, except where foot noted, or otherwise noted.

FOR THE RECORD: THE TESTIMONIES OF MARY MAGDALENE AND JUDAS ISCARIOT
Second Edition

Copyright © 2024, 2025 by Cynthia Farrar Burse.

Paperback: ISBN 979-8-9923986-0-1

Library of Congress Control Number: 2025901382

Cover image: Canva. Used by permission.

Cover Design: Cynthia Farrar Burse

---

The contents of this book are protected by U.S. copyright laws, and all rights are reserved. Except for brief quotations in critical articles, reviews or sermons, no part of this book may be reproduced in any manner without prior written permission from the publisher.

To request permission, contact the publisher at:resilience976@gmail.com.

Exact scripture quotations are taken from the ESV® Bible (The Holy Bible, English Standard Version®), copyright © 2001 by Crossway, a publishing ministry of Good News Publishers. Used by permission. All rights reserved.

Unless otherwise noted, biblical quotations are the author's rendition of various biblical translations.

Printed by IngramSpark. Corrected file updated 1/26/26.

Published by Cynthia Farrar Burse, Columbus, OH

This book was written to aid and abet the work of Yeshua of Nazareth, and to encourage offenders everywhere.

Honor is accorded to my late grandfather, Rev. Felix Festus Bryan, whom I never knew; my late grandmother, Laney Odessa Smith Bryan Ward, who knew what I would become long before I did; and to my late great-aunt Olivia Marie Bryan Birchette, a heavenly angel who walked the Earth as a mortal being.

The gift of gratitude is extended to my editor, Dr. Joya Stevenson, for guiding me so expertly through the initial drawing-out process; my New Testament seminary professor, Dr. David Rensberger, for leading me out of interpretive darkness into exegetical light; and my friend and colleague, Rev. Dr. Brian K. Blount, for being a truth-teller about the state of the human condition.

Book Contents

# Personal Thoughts

Inside a box in my closet is an elementary school photo of me standing between a fellow student, a boy whose name I cannot recall, and Miss Lynch, the school librarian. Standing behind my classmate and me is the school principal, whose face I can vividly recall but not her name, and everyone is smiling for the camera. In front of us is a square wooden table on which sit two tall stacks of books, one belonging to my schoolmate and the other to me. The photograph was part of a local newspaper article highlighting student summer reading accomplishments and promoting the joy of reading.

My love of reading is why I spent many nights hiding under my bedsheet in a tepee-like cocoon—book in one hand and flashlight in the other—reading when I should have been sleeping and ignoring calls from the floor below to "Turn that light off!" Most Saturdays, after doing my chores, I would make the two to three-mile hike to the library downtown to refresh my reading material, always maintaining the same routine. I'd cross the 34th Street bridge,[1] return the books read the previous week, spend two or three hours wandering down rows and rows of bookcases, check out more books for the week ahead and then head back home. Rarely did I venture out of the house without a book, in case a reading opportunity presented itself. Or, to distract myself from the adult world going on around me.

But had my first-grade teacher, the late Mrs. Celestine Dobson,[2] not noticed and addressed my word list poverty (reading deficiency), things might have turned out much differently for me. Mrs. Dobson not

---

[1] My other option was the more distant 28th Street bridge. Both bridges are in Newport News, Virginia, and exist courtesy of the national public policies and state institutional practices that facilitated racial and economic segregation.
[2] Mrs. Dobson was my teacher at Booker T. Washington Elementary School, and we were both members of Carver Memorial Presbyterian Church.

only taught me how to spell and pronounce words, she taught me how to learn using the aid of a dictionary and to read with the goal of understanding in mind. She made me feel as though I could accomplish anything. This shout-out is my public display of gratitude and thanksgiving to Mrs. Dobson for teaching me to read for myself, the ancestor of being able to think for myself.

Books are gateways into other worlds where I can meet people I will never actually meet, transported to places I will never visit, and am challenged by perspectives I could never have imagined on my own. iPad and IPhones notwithstanding, there's something plain and uncomplicated about holding a book in my hand and turning the pages with my fingers.

Reading the Bible is an experience of its own, like visiting the house of my own soul, and it is, my humble opinion, *the* book described by Oscar Wilde—the one worth reading again and again. Because with each fresh reading deeper meaning and understanding emerge, the memory of GOD begins coming into view, and healing from the separation[3] takes place. The Bible is a sacred book because GOD desires that all should hear and know GOD's testimonies for themselves, and it uses written words as symbols of symbols to guide people into an awareness of GOD's love and presence.

You may be nodding and agreeing to what I have written thus far. If you are one of the tens of thousands, perhaps hundreds of thousands, of people who once took a Bible in hand, went to the local

---

[3] Genesis 1:1,3; Exodus 4:12; Psalms 23, 150; Isaiah 26:3-4, 41:10; Jeremiah 29:11-14; Micah 6:8; John 14:25-26.

church in search of GOD,[4] and were driven away by the teachings and/or members of the congregation (in the name of the God-in-the-Bible), you may feel and think very differently. You may see yourself as one among an exodus of people who have turned away from GOD, the Bible, the Church and anything any of them have to say.

Imagine that GOD is embarrassed by, and apologizes for, the hateful behavior done by people who profess to know and love GOD. Would that be enough to get you to consider giving GOD—the guarantor of second chances—a second chance?

What do you think about making time to read the Bible on your own?

Reading is a fundamental building block of education and beneficial to one's physical, mental, emotional and spiritual health. Clinical tests have proven that reading in general reduces mental decline by 32% in seniors (my cohorts), and that reading the Bible in particular lessens depression, anxiety and anger, and increases compassion, forgiveness and one's sense of purpose.[5]

If none of what I have said thus far resonates with you, how about this. Reading the Bible—and knowing for one's self what the Bible

---

[4] GOD, in contrast to the God-in-the-Bible, represents the unseen CREATOR, the energy force of creation which existed before a human design appeared, who will not and cannot be held hostage to or by the religious beliefs of any one nation, tribe, religious person or sect.

[5] Adam Macinnis, "Study: Trauma-Informed Bible Reading Reduces Depression, Anxiety and Anger," *Christianity Today*, May 3, 2021, https://www.christianitytoday.com/news/2021/may/bible-reading-study-trauma-ptsd-covid19-mental-health.html.

actually says—is not only as faithful a counterbalance to the inadequacies-of-religion[6] as one might possibly hope to be, it's the only way to validate whether the Bible actually says what someone else says it does, or to legitimately call into question a claim of biblical truth. This book is foot noted for validation purposes.

According to the Christian church's biblical truth, Judas Iscariot was a thief and the betrayer of Jesus of Nazareth, and Mary Magdalene was a prostitute healed of demonic possession by Jesus. As reported in the *Gospel of Judas* and the *Gospel of Mary*, respectively, Judas was Jesus' friend and Mary was the disciple Jesus loved the deepest. This discrepancy creates room for reasonable doubt about the accuracy of Christianity's allegations.

In *For the Record: The Testimonies of Mary Magdalene and Judas Iscariot*, the biblical stories concerning Mary Magdalene and Judas Iscariot are remembered and presented in a new way, having five goals in mind. Entertaining folks; helping readers become acquainted, reacquainted or better acquainted with the Bible; determining how a faith not governed by religious institutional rules and regulations looks and operates; reviving the passion and energy planted in the New Testament by the Holy Spirit[7]; and lessening the distance between GOD, the academy, the church pew and the back alley.

---

[6] I feel certain that the phrase "the inadequacies of religion" is sufficiently explicit. If not, it refers to all the things Jesus cautioned those leading the temple about (i.e., Matthew 23:13–36, "Woe to you . . .") in conjunction with all the similar and documented acts of unfaithfulness and wrongdoing performed by members and leaders in the church. The terms 'church' and 'Church' will be later defined.
[7] The "Spirit of (GOD's) Truth" described in Isaiah 11:2; Joel 2:28; Zechariah 4:6; John 14:26, 15:13-14; Acts 1:8, 2:4; Revelation 2:7 (et al).

To acknowledge His Lordship, all mentions of Jesus of Nazareth are uppercase, including pronouns. The exception being when both Mary and Judas testify of meeting Jesus for the very first time. To honor His personhood and in recognition of His Jewish roots, Jesus is addressed by His given Hebrew name, Yeshua. As a sign of respect for the sacredness with which the Jewish community holds the temple and Torah, and Christians hold the church and Bible, in many cases these terms are uppercase.

For the benefit of readers unfamiliar with the Bible, an alphabet positioned to the immediate right of a scripture verse (i.e. Joshua 2:1b) corresponds to its position in the verse. In other words, the letter *a* bears on the first sentence in a verse, *b* the second sentence, *c* the third sentence and so on. In the footnotes, scripture verses placed within parentheses identify the intended scripture text in its entirety. Mark 6:30–32 (30–44) is an example.

The following section, *Findings of Fact*, is an overview of the biblical details used by Christianity to support its accusations against Mary Magdalene and Judas Iscariot.

I hope readers will receive a great deal of enjoyment from reading this book. I hope equally that the findings-of-facts are compelling enough to inspire some hesitant readers to take a look—or a second look—at GOD, and that Mary's and Judas' testimonies lead many to consider giving GOD a second chance.

**Findings of Fact**

## Questions of Fact

According to the language of Law, questions-of-fact come into play when different parties disagree on the facts presented. Each party then produces evidence to support their version of the facts, or their truth. A trier or finder-of-fact, typically a jury or a judge, listens to and weighs all the evidence presented by both parties before deciding which facts meet the burden of proof beyond a reasonable doubt, by a preponderance (or greater part) of the evidence, or by clear and convincing evidence. In this Findings of Fact section, the evidence—or facts—presented by the Christian church to corroborate its allegations against Mary Magdalene and Judas Iscariot is examined and cross-examined, with additional information presented on behalf of Judas and Mary—for the record.

## Making the Case

The term Bible is best understood according to the faith tradition of its reader. Judaism, for example, refers to the biblical canon as the Tanakh[8] (or Hebrew Bible in English), which many people still refer to as the Old Testament. Traditional Christianity and Messianic Judaism[9] consider the Bible to consist of both the Hebrew Bible and the New Testament, with or without the apocrypha, a term harvested from the Greek word *apokryphos*, meaning hidden or secret things. As a rule, the term apocrypha refers to fourteen specific books of ancient Jewish

---

[8] The Tanakh is composed of three sections: Torah (Instruction or Law), Nevi'im (Prophets), and Ketuvim (Writings).
[9] Messianic Judaism believes Yeshua/Jesus of Nazareth to be GOD'S promised Messiah, or Savior, as does Christianity, but in most other ways Messianic Jews maintain their Jewish heritage and many of its traditions.

and Christian literature that exist outside the canonical,[10] or authorized, Bible. If the list of books expanded, so that it included other extra-biblical texts, the Gospel of Mary and Gospel of Judas would certainly qualify as appropriate for inclusion as apocrypha. A separate fact worth mentioning is that throughout history and across generations, faith traditions and individuals of faith have disagreed with, dismissed or rejected certain portions of the Bible, without altering its status as a sacred record.[11] For these reasons, understanding the Bible is according to the faith tradition of its reader.

Turning individual books, letters and other manuscripts into a collection known as the New Testament took multiple church councils and several centuries to complete, with many of the items identified as unacceptable for inclusion. The primary justification given by the councils for preserving such a clear boundary line was that the extra-biblical scriptures were extraneous. To phrase it differently, church leaders responsible for choosing which books to include in the New Testament regarded their approved selections as written under the divine inspiration of GOD's Holy Spirit. The rejected scripture texts, not so much.

---

[10] The term "canonical" refers to a very specific collection of books and scriptures that make up the Hebrew Bible and New Testament in our possession today. All other religious scriptures and books fall under the heading of "extra-biblical" (outside of the Bible) texts.

[11] The tradition of Marcionism, for example, accepted some portions of the New Testament while denying the Bible's claim that Jesus was fully human and rejecting the 'violent God' of the Hebrew Bible. Howard Thurman wrote in *Jesus and the Disinherited* (1976, p. 31) that his grandmother would not allow him to read anything to her that was attributed to the Apostle Paul because of Ephesians 6:5 (ESV). "Slaves, obey your earthly masters with fear and trembling . . ." She told her grandson, "I promised my Maker that if I ever learned to read and if freedom ever came, I would not read that part of the Bible."

An interesting fact about ancient extra-biblical texts is that they tended to challenge the church's sanctioned views concerning the life of Jesus and GOD's salvation story. This fact matters because what was true in times past remains true today—anyone challenging the church's authority and doctrine or holding opinions and teachings too contrary to what the church finds acceptable, is at risk of being pushed to the margin, which was the outcome for the Gospel of Mary and the Gospel of Judas.

As a counselor and teaching device, the Bible does an excellent job of summarizing GOD's interest in behavior over professed belief, laying out the conditions undergirding the "if you . . . then I will" nature of divine promises, and revealing the intended inheritances for both the criminal (excuse me, sinner) concerned about these matters and the one who is not. The Bible also functions like any other book in that it uses words to paint descriptive pictures, reveal information and tell stories about different places, events and people—or characters. The problem with being a character in a book like the Bible is that the character's persona tends to remain fixed and established across time, just as the writer or author first portrayed them to be.

If a character in the story is presented and remembered as the proverbial 'good guy' that might not be such a bad trade-off. But, if his or her enduring legacy is one of perceived moral failings or criminality, that character is likely to be remembered first and foremost—and sometimes always—as the worst thing someone else judged or imagined them to be or to have done. The consequence being that one person's perception takes on a life of its own to become reality in the minds of generations of people.

Traditional Christian faith rightly accords a presumption of truth to all things written in the Bible, but faith is different from tangible evidence proving something said or written is true. For greater than 2,000 years now, the Christian church has portrayed Mary Magdalene as a prostitute who was healed of demonic possession by Jesus of Nazareth, and characterized Judas Iscariot as a thief who betrayed the whereabouts of Jesus in exchange for a certain amount of money, but are the accusations true?

As a body of evidence, the Bible is a *presumptive* record, meaning that the information contained within it—the stories, events, parables, conversations and so on—is presumed to be reliable enough to function as evidence until such time as the information is proven questionable, or untrue.

After the Gospel of Judas and the Gospel of Mary were uncovered in the Egyptian desert, translated by scholars and became available to the public, the time came to revisit the stories traditionally told about Judas Iscariot and Mary Magdalene. Because unlike the church, the communities who wrote those two gospels held Judas and Mary in high esteem.

The facts, as they currently stand, are these:

1. Scholars established long ago that the Bible is not one long, continuous and uninterrupted book written by one individual, but a compilation of assorted narratives and accounts composed and influenced by multiple human authors and editors, meaning that more than one person has handled or had access to the church's evidence

2. There is a glaring absence of any clear, convincing or demonstrative evidence to support the allegations made against Mary Magdalene and Judas Iscariot

3. Neither Mary nor Judas ever had the opportunity to face

their accusers, a clear violation of due-process

When these three independent facts are considered in tandem, room is created for the presence of reasonable doubt concerning the accuracy of the Church's accusations—and doubt about an accusation that cannot be substantiated by the available evidence is an accusation in need of being revisited, on the grounds that a possible miscarriage of justice may have taken place. In this book, with the aid of the Gospel of Judas, the Gospel of Mary, the Hebrew Bible, the New Testament and some imagination on my part, Judas and Mary finally get to have their say.

## The Church's Inception

Long before the construction of buildings called churches, Believers in Jesus of Nazareth were primarily a hodgepodge of Jews and Gentiles collectively known as people of the *Way*.[12] They met in one another's unassuming homes for worship, and practiced a radical sharing of resources whereby personal possessions were distributed according to an individual's or a family's need. Whether the people belonging to the Way chose to brand themselves that way or the term was assigned to them by others, the designation aligns with a statement in John 14:6 attributed to Jesus: "I am the way . . . no one comes to the Father except through me."

---

[12] Acts 4:34–35, 9:1–2, 19:9, 23, 22:4, 24:14, 22.

According to Acts 11:26, a congregation in Antioch under the leadership of Barnabas and Saul were the first to describe themselves as "Christian", a shift in identity that may have been a natural response to the title Jesus the Christ[13] that began circulating sometime after His execution.

In Acts 13:9, Saul undergoes his own change in identity. Thereafter, Saul is known by his Latin (or Roman) name—Paul—and it is Paul who is considered by many to be one of the most influential leaders of the early Christian church and author of a significant portion of the New Testament. It is for these reasons that whenever names of important church leaders have been counted, Paul's name has been at the top of the list, but according to the criteria laid down by Jesus,[14] Barnabas' name should be at the top of the roll call.

Saul was a Pharisaic Jew whose mission in life had been to execute as many people of the Way as he could find.[15] After an epiphany framed within a flash of light that blinded him,[16] Saul repented of his evil deeds and attempted to join Jesus' disciples as one of them, but they turned their backs on him, knowing his history. Only Barnabas was willing to have anything to do with Saul. It was Barnabas who invited Saul to accompany him to Antioch,[17] rather than the other way around as many imagine, and had it not been for Barnabas' commitment to follow the way of Jesus, who knows what would have become of the mighty Paul?

---

[13] Matthew 16:16; Mark 8:29; Luke 2:26–32, 4:41, 9:20; John 1:41, 11:27.
[14] Matthew 20:25–7, 23:10–12, 25:35; Mark 10:43–44.
[15] Acts 7:58, 8:1–3, 9:1–2, 22:4, 19–20.
[16] Acts 22:6.
[17] Acts 9:26–27, 11:22, 25–26.

However, when Saul received the opportunity to do for someone else what Barnabas had done for him—to take a man with a poor reputation under his wing and mentor him—he refused to do it, judging the man (Mark) as unworthy. Saul chose instead to mentor Silas, a man other men approved of, while Barnabas took Mark under his supervision and went on his way.[18] Nevertheless, Paul's name is the one celebrated across the generations, while Barnabas' name faded into a historical footnote. Two more examples (in addition to Judas and Mary) of biblical characters remembered according to how someone else imagined them to be.

What I wonder most is, did Saul rebrand himself as Paul in order to minimize or hide his reputation and history as a persecutor, prosecutor and executioner of people belonging to The Way? Was Saul attempting to minimize his Jewishness in favor of cultivating and strengthening his Roman citizenship to connect better with Gentiles, to Saul's advantage? What—really—was his motivation for changing his name?

Many scholars agree that by the close of the second century, all the books contained in the New Testament as we now have it had been written and were circulating among different communities, and the formal church leadership structure of bishops, priests, and deacons mentioned throughout the latter portion of the New Testament was in place and fully operational.

Sometime around 313 CE, after enduring more than two centuries of hostility and persecution in Rome, Christianity gained legal

---

[18] Acts 15:36–40.

status within the Roman Empire through an agreement called the Edict of Milan, and Emperor Constantine I became the first Roman emperor to convert to the Christian faith. Some scholars and theologians argue he did so for the intended purpose of using Christianity as the Roman Empire's political propaganda machine, while others insist he converted to the faith in response to a religious epiphany. Whatever the reason, and following his conversion, Constantine ordered a group of Christian bishops to begin the process of institutionalizing faith in Jesus, work that was completed by the Council of Rome sometime during the fourth century (circa 382 CE). Thereafter, Christianity became the official religion of Rome and religious voice of authority for the Roman Empire.

During the sixth century, Roman Catholicism and the doctrine of spiritual authority through apostolic succession emerged, the process by which Peter the disciple was officially designated "father" of the church. In the Great Schism of 1054, the church divided itself into Eastern and Western branches. The consequence of doctrinal and political disagreements over what images should occupy what place in the sanctuary, who the leader of the church actually was, and other matters.

In the sixteenth century, a group of Western clergymen used the power of the printing press to challenge several church doctrines they felt did not honor the teachings of Jesus. Scholars are still debating whether their intent was to reform the church from the inside or revolt against it. One of the most crucial theological issues the clergy demanded be addressed was the selling of indulgences, a monetary payment given to the church by a sinner (or a sinner paying on another sinner's behalf) in exchange for future salvation and forgiveness of sin. The revolt—or protest—against this practice became known as the Protestant Reformation.

The outcome of the reformation was the splintering of the western branch of the Christian church into Roman Catholicism and Protestantism, triggering wars and persecutions that continue to this day in certain parts of the world. In response to the Protestant Reformation, Catholicism used a counter-reformation to fight what it called heresy, schism, blasphemy and false doctrine, terms Protestantism subsequently updated to include apostasy, error, godlessness, dissension, unbelief, free-thinking, protest, and difference. Two thousand-plus years later, the church now has billions of Christians separated into thousands upon thousands of denominations, sects and faith communities.

Throughout this book, the institutionalized faith in Jesus as described above is the intended meaning of the term 'church'.

## The Church and Its Love Affair with Sin

Presbyterianism is the Protestant branch of the Church in which my maternal grandfather, my cousin Sheila and I have served as ordained clergy. The tradition is rooted in the works of a sixteenth-century French minister and theologian named John Calvin, one of several clergy members who led the Protestant Reformation. Among Calvin's most significant contributions to the church was his theory concerning *total depravity*, a theory debated, affirmed and rejected by several other theologians and scholars.

Calvin's understanding was founded on his belief that all of humankind is "naturally depraved and faulty [and that] nothing appears within or around us that has not been contaminated by great immorality [due to] the woman's unfaithfulness and [because the man] turned aside to falsehood."[19] While Calvin's perspective and rationales invite debate, his overall theology is correct. We are all guilty of having committed some immoral or dishonest wrongdoing in word, thought and/or behavior, which Christianity has traditionally articulated using the phrase "all are sinners."

Some Christians believe that means an ongoing and unchanging state of being, but that interpretation feels irreconcilable with GOD's promise to delete and cancel crimes and offenses so that "sin is remembered no more."[20] Why, then, should all people everywhere always be referred to as sinners? A clearer, less abstract and less ambiguous idiom might be to say, "We're all criminals."

An accusation of sin is easy to make and easier still to deny, given that sinfulness is generally defined according to an individual's or group's religious opinion and affiliation, but the law makes it much more difficult to dismiss accusations and charges of criminal behavior. Accusations of alleged crimes typically lead to an inquest—or an inquisition in the court of public opinion—particularly when a crime has clearly taken place, and the individual denying involvement or responsibility was clearly involved. If guilt is established (regardless of the actual truth), the law then becomes that individual's primary decision maker.

---

[19] John Baillie, John T. McNeil, and Henry P. Van Dusen, eds., *Calvin: Institutes of the Christian Religion*, Vol. 1 (Philadelphia: Westminster Press: 1960), 254, 38, 245. Notice how much more derogatory the blame assigned to the woman is.
[20] Isaiah 43:25; Jeremiah 31:34; Micah 7:19; 2 Colossians 1:13–14; Hebrews 8:12, 10:17–18; 1 John 1:9.

An otherworldly similarity exists between the world's criminal legal system, where crimes, verdicts and sentences are recorded, and the heavenly criminal court system mentioned in Revelation 20:12. Open before GOD are the Book of Life (of the Lamb that was slain) and books containing the names, crimes, verdicts and sentences of people whose names are not mentioned in the Book of Life. When viewed from this perspective, it makes little sense to say "all are sinners" because the presence of the Book of Life lying separate and apart from the many other books signifies and clarifies that sin cannot hold hands with GOD. Nor is it likely a sinner would be able to stand boldly before GOD's throne.[21]

Many crimes committed on Earth generally seem to go unnoticed, unreported and unpunished—like most sin, as though it never happened—but GOD, looking down from on high, sees it all.

Evidence of criminality for some is on a tax form submitted to the IRS that was not entirely truthful, a federal crime known as tax fraud. Other folks have committed adultery (a felony in some states and a misdemeanor in others), executed illegal U-turns, driven above the posted speed limit, taken items from work without permission, concealed a colleague or coworker's wrongdoing, embezzled other people's money, committed murder, predatory lending, rape, healthcare fraud, or other acts of physical or economic violence. These are just some of the crimes being committed on a daily basis, either by the person peering back at us in the mirror or by someone we pass while strolling down the street on any given day. It may be difficult for humans to discern or determine a state of sinfulness in others, but from the partial list above, it is evident

---

[21] Revelation 13:8; Hebrew 4:16.

that most every person is a criminal according to the law, and this is true regarding GOD's laws as well.

The challenge for those of us who have (thus far) managed to avoid becoming a *convicted* criminal is resisting the temptation to minimize personal wrongdoing(s) by judging, comparing or ranking our own criminal activities against the wrongdoings and crimes committed by others. As many in the church rank and compare sins, guided by the mistaken belief that one type has a more favorable status before GOD than another type.

Criminality in the Bible is easier to identify in some passages than in others. Cain's crime of murdering Abel comes to mind (Genesis 4:8), as does King David's adultery with the wife of one of his most trusted soldiers (2 Samuel 11:2–4c), the unnamed assailants who beat and leave a man half-dead on the side of a road (Luke 10:30), and the shrewd but dishonest manager in Luke 16:1–8. Other crimes and criminals are not so clear. Consider Jacob's gain of great wealth at his father-in-law's/Uncle Laban's expense, for example, or Laban's repeated efforts to cheat and take advantage of Jacob (Genesis 29:15–25, 30:25–43). Who, really, is the thief—the perpetrator of criminal behavior—in this situation?

Likewise, in Mark 5:1–20 is the story of a physically and religiously unclean, homeless man tormented by demons who lives in a graveyard and engages in self-mutilation. On repeated occasions, the members of the local community attempt to restrain the man in shackles and chains, but each time he breaks free. Even in his demented state, he seemingly has enough presence of mind to reject being enslaved, raising multiple questions.

One wonders why the members of the community did not use their financial resources to address the factors creating the man's debilitated state, rather than spending it on shackles and chains trying to keep him locked up. What crime(s) had the man committed that warranted such violence against him? The text never says, but here is the most intriguing part of the story. While the tormented man remains in his state of brokenness, the community members never express any feelings of fear about being around him. It is only *after* Jesus comes along and levels the playing field that their fear is vocalized—fear not only of the man who has been made clean, is back in his right mind and ready to take his rightful place in the world, but fear also of Jesus.

Did the community members interpret the situation as, "Oh, no, this man has become our competition!"? Is it possible that, in his broken state, the man was a convenient means by which to compare and measure themselves? Did keeping him captive allow them to feel superior and better about themselves, and was Jesus sent away before He could do something similarly good for someone else? Given that the community had no reservations about acting violently against a man who was violent against no one but himself, the question of who the real criminal is in this situation—the community members or the man who was treated like one—remains unanswered.

The next two sections examine specific details with respect to Christianity's accusations against the legendary Mary Magdalene and the notorious Judas Iscariot.

<u>The Beloved Mary Magdalene</u>

Mary Magdalene's portrayal in this book is of a woman who went in search of something and did not rest until she found it. She is strong even as a child, and the imaginative portion describing the backdrop of her life reflects this. In adulthood, Mary is depicted not only in her traditional role as the first to see Jesus' resurrected body, but also as an authentic apostle of Jesus and the "beloved" disciple and "son" mentioned in John 19:26. What's more, in her testimony, Mary sheds light on the cryptic saying of Jesus to the disciple Peter. "If my will is that [s]he remain right here until I come [again], what business is that of yours?"[22]

Although the Gospel of Mark and Gospel of Luke agree that Mary was reportedly possessed by demons (and I can think of a few demon-possessed days of my own), Luke asserts the same thing was being said about Jesus and all the other women traveling with Him.[23] Having said that, no text anywhere in the New Testament associates Mary Magdalene with prostitution. If the accusation were true the absence of any mention of it would be exceptional, given the ease with which the Bible reports Rahab's prostitution (Joshua 2:1b) and Gomer's promiscuity and whoredom (Hosea 1:2–3d). In the same manner—and notwithstanding the oral traditions preserved by the church—no scriptural evidence exists to support either the supposition of Mary Magdalene as the unidentified sinner woman who washed Jesus's feet (Luke 7:36–38). Nor as the unnamed woman about to be stoned to death after being caught in adultery with an unmentioned and unnamed man (John 8:3–11). The remaining texts mentioning Mary Magdalene by

---

[22] John 21:22.
[23] Matthew 12:22–24; Mark 16:9; Luke 8:2–3, 11:14–15.

name are associated with her presence at the crucifixion, death and resurrection of Jesus.

The earliest authors of Matthew, Mark, Luke and John all agree that Mary was present at the tomb after the resurrection of Jesus took place, although they disagree with one another whether other women were also present and who those women were.[24] Whether one or many, the consensus of all the gospel writers is that women were the first to receive and proclaim the good news about Jesus' resurrection. Mark tempers, or scorns, this honor by commenting that the poor women were too frightened to tell anyone the news (16:8). Luke disagrees, stating the women *did* share the resurrection news but that none of the male disciples who heard it believed either the message or the messengers. It was, they said, pure female nonsense (24:10–11).

The gospel accounts also contradict Paul's testimony that Peter was the first person to see Jesus in His resurrected state. In fact, Paul makes no mention whatsoever of any women being present at, or associated with, the resurrection—not even Mary Magdalene.[25] Peter opposes Mary as well. According to the Gospel of Mary, he is so disturbed by the depth and intimacy of her relationship with Jesus that he publicly denounces her personhood and advises the other disciples to doubt her reliability and the truthfulness of her words because—wait for it—she's a woman.[26]

---

[24] Matthew 28:1; Mark 16:1; Luke 23:55–24:1, 10; John 20:1.
[25] 1 Corinthians 15:3–5.
[26] Karen L. King, "The Gospel of Mary with the Greek Gospel of Mary," *The Nag Hammadi Scriptures: The Revised and Updated Translation of Sacred Gnostic Texts, Complete in One Volume*, ed. Marvin Meyer (New York: HarperCollins, 2007), 744.

What matters most to Mary is carrying out the duties of faithfulness, receiving the rewards of faith and reveling in the love of Jesus. Through her testimony, Mary becomes the embodiment of what it means to become fully human. She applies the lessons life presents to her, becomes a useful vessel for GOD's purposes and finds love in the process.

At first glance, portraying Mary Magdalene as the beloved disciple might seem like a bit of a stretch—an implausible option even— given that John 20:1–2 identifies Mary and "the one whom Jesus loved" as two distinct individuals, but my conjecture is not an untried idea. Grounded in part in the work of biblical scholars Ramon Jusino and the late Esther de Boer.

According to Jusino, the "positive contributions made by women to the development of the early church have been minimized throughout history. There was a concerted effort on the part of the male leadership of the early church to suppress the knowledge of any major contributions made by female disciples . . . [and] much of Mary Magdalene's legacy fell victim to this suppression." Prominent female disciples, Jusino asserts, "quickly became an embarrassment to the male leaders of the emerging institutional church."[27] Consequently, Mary's influential leadership role in her community created problems for those wanting to become part of the up-and-coming church institution, because they implicitly understood a woman leading a ministry would never be acceptable to those responsible for organizing the Christian Church.

---

[27] Ramon K. Jusino, "Mary Magdalene: Author of the Fourth Gospel?", 1998, accessed September 16, 2020, https://ramon_k_jusino.tripod.com/Magdalene.pdf, 2, 3.

Jusino maintains this dilemma was resolved using two separate strategies. Step one: those wanting to be included as members of the church customized their own belief systems to better "conform to the teachings of the emerging church hierarchy." Step two: An anonymous male disciple was inserted into the resurrection scene (John 20:2–8) to introduce confusion into the text so that going forward, Mary and the beloved disciple ("the one whom Jesus loved") would be interpreted as two different people. Her position as "the true founder and hero of . . . the Johannine community" could then be disguised and her biblical presence watered down and minimized. In Jusino's reasoned opinion, the version of the Gospel of John in our possession today "is the work of an editor belonging to the group which aligned itself with the institutional church."[28]

Scholar Esther de Boer concurs with the interpretation of Mary Magdalene as the beloved disciple. She argues, "Mary Magdalene is concealed in the male anonymous disciple."[29] De Boer's position differs from Jusino's in that she does not attribute the concealment to the work of a redactor or editor. From her perspective, "a repressive atmosphere with regard to women is fundamental to the Gospel of John as a whole, disclosing a repressive environment [even] within the Johannine community, which corresponds to the [oppressive] one outside."[30] In

---

[28] Jusino, "Mary Magdalene," 2, 4, 7; John 20:2.
[29] Esther A. de Boer, "Mary Magdalene and the Disciple Jesus Loved," http://www.lectio.unibe.com, January 2000, 2. A number of scholars assert that Mary Magdalene was the initial author of the Gospel of John and de Boer supports this view as well.
[30] Ibid.

other words, the biased attitudes toward women present and active in society in general and in the emerging institutional church in particular, were also present in Mary's beloved community.

In this book, and despite the masculine Greek grammar,[31] Mary Magdalene is a "son" to Jesus' mother, a kinship borrowed from the relationship that existed between Hebrew biblical characters Naomi and Ruth. When the elderly Naomi is widowed and all her sons have died, her daughter-in-law Ruth pledges to stay by her side always, a decision commended by the other women in the community who single Ruth out as being of more value to Naomi "than seven sons."[32] De Boer appears to support a Mary-as-son interpretation as well, contending that by not assigning or adding a masculine address to "Behold your mother" (John 19:27), the disciple being addressed is "to *represent* [Jesus] as a son."[33]

Mary Magdalene's authentic character (like that of Barnabas') flies so low under the radar that it's easy to understand why many people tend to see only what other people designed for them to see. Mary as nothing special at all, just one incidental character among many in GOD's salvation story, rather than a leading one.

Judas Iscariot—Betrayer or Friend?

The Gospel of Judas (referencing Judas Iscariot) was uncovered—or rediscovered—in the 1970s, but second-century church

---

[31] "Γύναι, ἴδε ὁ υἱός σου" ("Woman, behold the son of you"; John 19:26).
[32] Ruth 4:15.
[33] De Boer, "Mary Magdalene," 5. (Emphasis) added.

bishop Irenaeus mentions the existence of the gospel.[34] The allegation of theft against Judas is becomes possible in part because he was the keeper of the disciples' community moneybag and, in part, because one solitary voice in the Bible accuses him of stealing.[35]

Two of the four gospels mention Judas' death but do not agree on how his life ends. The rumor circulating in Matthew's community was that Judas returned the quid pro quo money to the Jewish high priest and hung himself. A different community was led to believe Judas purchased a field with the thirty-coin payoff, then committed suicide by throwing himself down on something so piercing his bowels gushed out,[36] proof to many medieval and contemporary clergy persons that Judas was a man in deep despair. These variations suggest that as reports of Judas' death began spreading from one community to the next, different tellers of the story rearranged the details, or added others at will. Case in point. According to Matthew 27:7, it was Jewish authorities who purchased a field with the money, not Judas, but what all four gospels *do* agree on is that Judas traded information about Jesus of Nazareth in exchange for a certain amount of money.[37]

The unexpected twist is that the Gospel of Judas also confirms what the four gospel writers contend—that Judas was directly involved

---

[34] Johannes van Oort, "Irenaeus's Knowledge of the Gospel of Judas: Real or False? An Analysis of the Evidence in Context," *HTS Teologiese Studies/Theological Studies* 69(1), May 6, 2013, 1 http://dx.doi.org/10.4102/hts.v69i1.1916.
[35] John 12:6.
[36] Matthew 27:3–5; Acts 1:18.
[37] Matthew 10:4, 26:16, 27:3; Mark 3:19, 14:10–11; Luke 6:16; John 6:71, 12:4, 13:21.

in, and was in some way responsible for, Jesus' arrest. The discrepancy
between the New Testament's portrayal of Judas as a betrayer[38] and the
Gospel of Judas' portrayal of him as Jesus' friend is subject to the
context employed and how Bible translators have chosen to handle the
Greek word *paradidōmi*.

Many English words are polysemous—words having multiple
meanings—and this capacity exists in other languages as well. The Greek
root of polysemous is *polysemos*, meaning "of many senses". In some
instances, the primary meaning of different words are sometimes so
similar they are freely interchangeable. Either one could be used in a
sentence with no loss of comprehension or understanding. For words that
cannot be freely interchanged in this way, the decision about what
meaning or definition to use usually defaults to context, the surroundings
and circumstances of any given situation.

In the case of Judas Iscariot, New Testament translators seem to
have chosen to translate *paradidōmi* using its third subordinate
definition, betray, rather than employing either of its two primary
meanings. 1. The act of transferring someone into the possession of
another,[39] as conveyed in Matthew 20:19, and 2. To deliver one up to

---

[38] Acts 1:17 seems to imply or acknowledge the possibility of Judas as friend
rather than betrayer. Cephas (Peter) affirms Judas as being "numbered" among
the twelve who would be awarded his share of reward. Verse 18, a sidebar entry,
makes certain the reader never forgets Judas's reported "wickedness."
[39] Horst Balz and Gerhard Schneider, *Exegetical Dictionary of the New
Testament*, Vol. 3 (Grand Rapids: Eerdmans, 1994), 18, 154. "Paradidōmi" is
defined in part as "the act whereby something or someone is transferred into the
possession of another; to entrust/commend/give for safekeeping; to hand over an
area of authority/authorize/permit; to hand over for judgment/punishment . . .

custody to be judged, condemned, punished, scourged, tormented, and put to death,[40] all of which is recorded as having happened to Jesus. In contrast, the word generally employed to signify the meaning of a traitor or betrayer is *prodótēs*,[41] as in Luke 6:16.

Although paradidōmi and prodótēs are not similar in either spelling or pronunciation, and both have different primary or cardinal[42] definitions, Bible translators have deemed the words similar enough to feel comfortable using the primary meaning of prodótēs for paradidōmi, a behavior I've termed *translation by consensus*.[43] In Judas' case, the impropriety of doing so becomes visible when the context as described in the Gospel of Judas becomes visible within the New Testament gospel narratives, which Judas describes in his testimony. The church's allegation of betrayal against Judas, when considered from the viewpoint of the Gospel of Judas, is unmerited. Judas did not betray Jesus, he handed Jesus over to the authorities, just as Jesus reportedly said would happen (Matthew 20:18b).

---

[which] is a threat to the one [being handed over] but follows a prescribed course."

[40] "G3860," Greek Dictionary (Lexicon-Concordance), lexiconcordance.com/3860.html, accessed June 24, 2024. See comparable description in Matthew 20:18–19.

[41] Acts 7:52 uses the word prodoté (betray); 2 Timothy 3:4 (ESV) translates the word as "treacherous" while the NKJV uses "traitor."

[42] Cardinal, another polysemous word, is also the name of a bird.

[43] Defined here as "the cooperative decision of Bible translators to replace the meaning of one word or phrase with the meaning of a similar, but not freely interchangeable, word or phrase for altruistic or other purposes."

The official act of being arrested, then handed over into the custody of authorities, can be a dangerous situation for the one being arrested and handed over,[44] but the acts themselves—the arrest and handing over—follow a predetermined course of events. By applying this line of thinking to the arrest scene in the Garden of Gethsemane—when the Gospel of Judas narrative is integrated in the New Testament gospels—the image emerging is that of the garden functioning as an *arranged* meeting place.

Consider this point as well. Jesus was a self-determined Man, meaning He did not allow other people to make decisions for Him or to decide His destiny. John 10:17–18 (ESV) confirms as much. "I freely lay down my life, just as I am free to take it up again—but no one *takes* it from me." Matters concerning Jesus would proceed according to His time, place and plan, but He needed help putting His plan into motion, someone He could trust to do what needed to be done. The Gospel of Judas indicates that someone was Judas Iscariot, a man I believe demonstrated strength of character, bravery in the face of certain defeat, and faithful loyalty to Jesus.

I have asked myself on numerous occasions why Judas was singled out and branded the betrayer of Jesus. Peter, for example, swore on his life that he would never leave Jesus' side, even on the threat of death, and the other ten male named disciples committed to do the

---

[44] Examples of others who experienced a dangerous handover include Eleanor Northington; Roderick Brooks; Ronald Green; Dyonta Quarles, Jr.; Akeem Terrell; Keenan Anderson; Irvo Otieno; Crystalline Barnes; and George Floyd.

same.[45] Nevertheless, when his personal association with Jesus posed a threat to his own life and well-being, Peter denied even knowing Him. Not once, but on three separate occasions.[46] Moreover, three times during the hours leading up to His arrest, Jesus asked Peter, James and John to pray for Him and three times found them sleeping instead,[47] and as Jesus was being taken into custody, every single one of the disciples abandoned Him and ran away.[48] Everyone except Judas, leading me to ask this question. Should not the actions of Peter, and the other ten disciples, be considered acts of betrayal in their own right?

Was Judas really a thief, as one lone voice in the Bible says he was? Could it be that someone planted evidence to make it appear as though he was? Whose agenda, really, was behind the personal attack on Judas in John 12:6, regarding his motive and opportunity for theft, and where is the evidence?

<u>A Note of Interest Concerning the Church and the Gospel of John</u>

Ramon Jusino, building on remarks made by scholar Raymond Brown, says there is a decisive connection between the Gospel of John and a religious movement known as Gnosticism.

Jusino writes that according to Brown, a majority in the Johannine community were Secessionists who had in their possession a pre-canonical version of the Gospel of John, which they shared with

---

[45] Matthew 26:30–35; Mark 14:26–31; Luke 22:31–34 (See also Zechariah 13:7).
[46] Matthew 26:69–75; Mark 14:66–72; Luke 22:54–62; John 18:15–17, 25–27.
[47] Matthew 26:40, 43–45; Mark 14:37, 40–41; Luke 22:45.
[48] Matthew 26:56b; Mark 14:50.

other faith communities such as the Gnostics, Docetists and Montaniests. Other biblical scholars have also put forth the idea that the Gnostic community was the faith tradition responsible for writing both the Gospel of Judas and the Gospel of Mary,[49] but there is ongoing theological debate about this matter as well. Central to Gnostic belief was the idea of transcendence or supernatural knowledge (*gnosis* in Greek) as the way to GOD. Among the Gnostic community were individuals who wanted to become part of the emerging institutional church.

How the Gospel of John, embraced by Gnostics, became part of the canonical Bible is a note of particular interest. Scholar Elaine Pagels maintains that "orthodox opposition" was poised to reject including the Gospel of John into the Bible. They eventually agreed to include it as part of a larger strategic plan involving John 14:6, "I am the way, the truth, and the life. No one comes to the Father except through me" (ESV). Pagels writes, "By indicating that one finds God only through Jesus, the saying, in its contemporary context, implies that one finds Jesus only through the church."[50] Phrased differently, orthodox church leaders determined that John 14:6 would be useful for fostering their theological belief that one *must* be a Christian to be saved from sin, a belief still prevalent among Christianity today.

My take on the text is that it clarifies the matter for everyone, because it states outright that it is Jesus alone who gets to decide who is in, who is out, and who gets to hang and party with GOD.[51] So far, I have

---

[49] Jusino, "Mary Magdalene," 7.
[50] Elaine Pagels, *The Gnostic Gospel* (New York: Vintage Books, 1979), 119.
[51] John 3:35.

yet to run across any scriptures suggesting Jesus plans to consult with the institutional church about His decisions.

What This Book Is and Is Not

In this book, my attention was on creating and constructing a shared human experience rather than an authentic Jewish background, because meaning comes out of experience. I have also attempted to write in such a way as not to perpetuate or incite groundless and misinformed anti-Semitic views. Scripture texts are intended to emphasize and highlight how more alike than different the Institutional Church and Temple are, not to cast blame on "the Jews".

This book is not an academic work, nor (intentionally) intended to be an academic resource. At its core, *For the Record: The Testimonies of Mary Magdalene and Judas Iscariot* is an interpretation of biblical stories written by a retired Protestant clergyperson as mainstream reading material for general audiences. Having said that, my aspiration was to incorporate the work of biblical and other scholars into the book in ways readers would find interesting, and that would help narrow the gap between GOD, the academy, the church pew and the back alley. My imagination limited only by the confines of first-century possibilities.

However, let me rush on to say that the information and stories in this book are examined interpretations, using the standards of *hermeneutics* and *exegesis.*

Biblical hermeneutics uses various methods and processes to understand a given scripture text according to the historical (or actual) bible writer's intent. Some of these methods include identifying the historical or cultural context of a text; studying the grammar and history of words used in the text; establishing what, if any, relationship exists between the words; and many other methods and processes as well.

Exegesis provides the interpretation and meaning, in part by harmonizing hermeneutical data with the biblical text. In contrast, biblical *isogesis* (or eisegesis) is an interpretation of the Bible constructed on personal beliefs, biases and agendas that read into (or attribute to) the Bible something not actually written in it.

My own hermeneutical process began with listening to the Spirit of GOD. The second step involved investigation, or the exercise of seeking and applying science and rationality to the Bible, made possible by the excellent resource materials written by scholars and others. The final step in my hermeneutical process was to deliberately and thoughtfully apply and connect the examined-world-of-the-Bible to the contemporary and modern situation around me. Stated differently, the limited and rational thinking and reasoning normally associated with interpretation of the Bible, I sometimes overruled in favor of imagination, faith, hope and love.

I liken the hermeneutical and exegetical processes to an archaeological dig, where excavators and archaeologists use specific tools to uncover buried treasures and communities one layer at a time. As biblical scholars and others use hermeneutical tools (methods and processes) to dig for exegetical understanding—one biblical location, word, community or character at a time. When the hermeneutical information is assembled and brought together, as bones of a dinosaur or ancient clay pot are reassembled, meaning and clarity take shape—or exegetically emerge—and when the Spirit of the Holy of Holies is added to this mix, the Bible becomes a living document.

No doubt, biblical scholars will agree with me that I have presented simplistic portrayals of what are very complex religious, philosophical and theological belief systems, including Christianity. Yet,

I would hope they could also agree that my exegetical interpretations are sound and my depictions reliably presented.

<u>Different and New</u>

The wonder and value of extra-biblical resources like the Gospel of Judas and the Gospel of Mary is that they serve as additional sources of authentic information pertaining to Jesus and the history of early Christianity, and they call attention to how genuinely alternative GOD really is.

Think about it.

What could be more unconventional than sending an unwed pregnant teenager (who religion has often vilified) and a convicted criminal (who most religious people do their best to avoid) as the portals through which to send forgiveness and salvation into the world? "I am doing something that has never been tried before, can you not see that?"[52] is how the God-of-the-Hebrew Bible phrases it. Language that not only conveys the potential for new possibilities but for new outcomes as well. An idea I hope is not lost on the church, which claims to be seeking what is ahead rather than what is behind,[53] what will be, rather than what has been or once was.

The idea of thinking differently and doing things in a new way can seem or even be exciting, but with newness and difference also come the unknown and the unfamiliar. "New" signals that the routine and

---

[52] Isaiah 43:18–19a.
[53] Philippians 3:13-14.

status quo are no more, no matter how things may appear at any given moment. GOD doing a new thing means that heaven's plans have changed and the order of things rearranged. As in the first will be last and the last will be first,[54] which is exactly what many in the ancient Jewish world during the time of Jesus did not want to hear and what many in the institutional church still have trouble believing. Because believing it means becoming entangled with people some in the Christian church would rather not know, and living out a faith demanding more than some might want to give, raising the question of who really, wants to be like Jesus?

As Judas prepares to take his seat in the witness chair, I find myself still asking these questions.

Were the labels applied to Mary Magdalene and Judas Iscariot—demon-possessed prostitute and betrayer and thief—someone's attempt to conceal or smear their real identities and contributions? Could it be that Peter, or Paul—or perhaps a different, anonymous church leader or scribe—tried to negatively influence how future readers and hearers would respond at the mere mention of Mary's and Judas' name? And, if the answer to any part of these questions is yes, who, from GOD's advantageous point of view, is the real offender and who is the injured party?

I invite you now into the courtroom where Judas and Mary finally get to have their say.

---

[54] Matthew 20:16.

# The Testimony of Judas Iscariot

## Judas' Appeal

*(Judas is sworn in by an officer of the court and takes his seat in the witness chair)*

Court official: "State your name for the record please."

Judas Iscariot, son of Simon.[55]

Judge: "Sir, the court has reviewed your case and found it to be a compelling one. The two charges imposed upon you by the Christian church are those of theft and betrayal. Your position is that evidence essential to your case was being hidden and suppressed, and that the absence of the evidence contributed to your conviction by the church and in the court of public opinion. In your brief to this Court, you also stated that the missing evidence is now in your possession and you wish now to testify on your own behalf. Is the Court correct in its understanding?"

The Court is correct, Your Honor.

Judge: "Very good. This is an unusual situation, sir, but the Court has consented to permit your testimony because it recognizes that justice requires more than a one-sided telling of what is a very complicated story. Please proceed when you're ready and take whatever time you need."

Thank you, Your Honor.

---

[55] John 13:2.

Before the Encounter

Before Rabbi Yeshua[56] of Nazareth came into my life, I was a very different kind of man. No, what I mean to say is, I lived a very different kind of life.

Before my branding as a thief and the worst of all men, people knew me to be an honorable, dependable and hard-working man, and I was proud to belong to a family who I thought valued and rewarded work done well. As the eldest of my father's many sons, I was heir to an empire that included sheep having a lineage stretching back to the time of Job and numbered ten times the quantity restored to him.[57]

My father's estate also generated income from breeding guard dogs, which many across Israel considered the finest watchdogs available. When my father entrusted me with the responsibility of training new pups, I knew it was his way of telling me how proud he was of me. It was easier for him to add to my responsibilities than it was to speak to me openly about his feelings. My mother was the one who possessed the gift of speaking encouraging words.

Work for me was more joy than labor because I enjoyed spending time with the animals, but it was also very important work. A well-trained guard dog standing between a flock of sheep or goats and a predator could mean the difference between success, bare survival or ruin, and this was especially true for families who had just a handful of livestock. When my father began donating pairs of watchdogs to families too poor to pay for them, I felt proud of him because I believed he

---

[56] "Yeshua" is the Hebrew form of Jesus, and in Jewish tradition, "Rabbi" is the equivalent of "Teacher," a title of respect.
[57] Job 42:12.

understood the gravity of their situation and wanted to help, as I did, and for a long time I believed this. Until I overheard my father say to his friend one day, "It's not my duty to maintain other people's standard of living! I am not a charity! There is serious money being made with every donation, believe me!" Then he laughed.

That day I heard my father speak those words, something inside me changed. I saw in him a man I never knew existed, and for the first time in my life wondered who my father really was, and who I was as his son. After that day, I felt ashamed of him and disappointed by him, but my shame and disappointment soon re-directed themselves toward me, because I was afraid to go to my father and hold him accountable for his words—too afraid of what doing so might cost me.

I said and did nothing, and everything went on just as it had before. I conformed to the expectations of others and obeyed the rules without complaint. Blending in so well with the traditions that had shaped me, that had it not been for our individual faces it would have been difficult to tell me apart from anyone else, but inside me was a growing sense of discontent for which there seemed to be no cure. I felt pressed down by my good life.

Then, Rabbi Yeshua of Nazareth came into my life and opened my eyes to the possibility that I did not have to live that way anymore.

## The Day of the Encounter

The day I first laid eyes on the Rabbi, my family and I were in Jerusalem for the holy days of Pesah.[58] The streets were so narrow and crowded with Jews and Gentiles,[59] it was next to impossible to walk without brushing up against someone. The air was crowded with voices, one shouting louder than the next in an effort to be heard above all the other noises. People hawking their wares, women negotiating prices, rabbis and students debating Law, the commotion of children at play, and beggars pleading for handouts with arms stretched out, but the noise was mild compared to the waste droppings littering the street. Discharge from the thousands of animals and birds for sell in the marketplace as pure sacrificial offerings. The smell was so overwhelming in some areas I was compelled to cover my nose and mouth while passing through, but these unsanitary conditions were of our own making. By 'our' I mean the ruling class to which my family and other elites belonged, for whom Passover was both a holy season and the perfect time to make a small fortune. The noise and smell were the results.

The number of pilgrims traveling to Jerusalem for Passover had been steadily increasing over many decades, even as the number of sacrificial animals available through neighboring supply chains steadily decreased. When it became clear that local suppliers could no longer keep up with Passover demand, the Temple priests put an industrial network in place linking the Temple directly with sellers who had

---

[58] Hebrew Pesaḥ (or Pesaḥ) or Jewish Passover.
[59] Gentiles are non-Israelites or non-Jews.

resources enough to meet the requirements of Passover but lived great distances away. The process was a simple one. Every year, wealthy landowners living along the most distant points of the network would pool their money together to pay special representatives to transport birds and livestock to Jerusalem in time for Pesah,[60] an arrangement that benefitted each of the participants in turn.

The priests were able to acquire a sufficient quantity of birds and livestock for Passover, and made a profit leasing retail space to the merchants. The merchants profited from selling the animals and birds to the public at cost-plus prices, and wealthy families like mine received the coveted priestly assurance that our religious obligations were satisfied. Eliminating the need to make a long and unpleasant journey to a crowded and untidy Jerusalem.

My father's household attended Passover every year for worship and religious reasons, yes, but also to ensure oversight of his investment. My role was to inspect the health of the transported livestock and keep an eye on the sales and profit portions belonging to my family's estate. I had just finished making my rounds and was walking away from the sheep pens in search of fresher air when I saw Rabbi Yeshua. To be exact, I saw a man dressed like a rabbi sitting alone in a corner of the temple square making a whip.

I found a spot on a wall to lean against that gave me an unobstructed view, and I stood there looking him over from head to toe

---

[60] Tia Ghose, "Animal Sacrifice at Temple Powered Ancient Jerusalem's Economy," NBC News, September 4, 2013, https://www.nbcnews.com/sciencemain/animal-sacrifice-temple-powered-ancient-jerusalems-economy-8C11073738. Animal slaughtering for sacrifices was the economic heart of Jerusalem.

and back again, wondering to myself what a rabbi was planning to do with a whip. I was surprised even more by how plain his manner of dress was. The coats worn by the rabbis in the privileged world where I once lived all had tzitzits—fringes—that were broad and wide, but those on the coat of the rabbi making the whip were narrow and short. The rabbis I knew all walked around with tefillah bound to both their hand and forehead even when not engaged in prayer, but the rabbi I was staring at wore none.[61]

His form and appearance had no attractive majesty or beauty— apart from skin the color of caramel, a thick mass of dark brown curls that fell just above his shoulders, and a look of pure determination on his face. At the time, I knew not whether the rabbi was being inspired by ambition, or GOD.

When I grew tired of standing, I moved to find a more comfortable place where I could sit and still keep the rabbi in sight. As he sat twisting cords together, he would sometimes stop and look around, as though taking in the scene. It happened often enough that I found myself looking around as well, trying to see our surroundings through his eyes.

The nation of Israel had been under the rule and control of foreign occupiers[62] for most of its existence, and the occupier's name at that time was the Roman Empire. The religious and political elite favored

---

[61] John 2:13-15. Tefillah is the leather box strapped to the left hand and forehead of Jewish rabbis. Four scriptural passages (Exodus 13:1–10, 13:11–16, Deuteronomy 6:4–9, 11:13–21) are contained in the forehead box, and in the hand box is one long scroll containing these same four scriptures. Also known as phylacteries. See Deuteronomy 6:8, 11:18; Matthew 23:5b; and Luke 8:44.
[62] For context, foreign occupiers included Assyria (732 BCE), Babylonia (598 BCE), Persia (536 BCE), and more recently, the Ottoman Empire (1517) and Britain (1917). In 1948, the state of Israel was re-established.

cooperation with Rome rather than resistance, with an eye on the rewards that came with being the emperor's friend. The priests were able to hold religious services and maintain temple customs without interruption, the half-Jewish king, Herod Antipas, had a throne he could pretend to call his own and wealthy aristocrats like my father received a free hand to run matters locally. So long as the conditions dictated by Rome were satisfied—law and order in the streets at all times, taxes paid to Caesar, and Caesar alone worshipped as Lord.

The presence of Roman soldiers with zero tolerance for rebels, agitators or public disruptions ensured that law and order were maintained, the responsibility for paying taxes fell mainly on the backs of the poor, and it was left to the priests, rabbis and other religious leaders to defend the case against worshipping anyone but GOD. To ensure the continuation of their status and benefits, the religious and social elite had an unwritten understanding of alliance. Should any hostility or disagreement that normally existed between them escalate to the point that the privileges, power or survival of either group were threatened, all differences would be put aside long enough to work together for the good and protection of all.

As a beneficiary of this arrangement, I had an up-close view of the self-serving ways of many priests and politicians. I saw also the depth of suffering endured by the poor who—in my eyes—possessed a resilience worthy of praise. They understood exactly what it was they needed, but the tragedy of poverty is there was only so much they could afford to do about anything.

When I turned to look again at the rabbi, he was standing in the middle of the street with his feet shoulder-width apart with a coiled whip in his hand. He threw his right arm so high into the air the entire whip uncoiled, and then quickly brought it down again. *CRACK!* The sound was so loud everyone standing nearby was shocked into stillness and silence. He began cracking the whip over his shoulders as he walked toward the merchants, and people fell over one another as they ran for cover. The rabbi shouted, "You've taken what GOD set apart as a sacred time of worship in the most sacred place on Earth and turned it and GOD's house of prayer into a common marketplace! Get out! Get your things and get out! Stop making my Father's house a place for your own profit!"[63]

He handled the whip with such skill it bordered on perfection, using it to drive the animals out of the marketplace, creating a stampede that turned over tables and sent money flying in every direction. Some of the merchants ran around trying to pick up the strewn coins, as others corralled birds and animals and the remainder rushed to surround and shout at the rabbi, demanding to know what right he had to shut them down.[64]

Not long after, Roman soldiers and the temple priests rushed to the scene to restore order. The chief priest set about trying to persuade the soldiers that the incident was under control, as other priests waved curious onlookers on their way with Passover greetings of "Chag same'ach!"[65] As though nothing out of the ordinary was going on and

---

[63] John 2:13–15a.

[64] John 2:15b–17 (Matthew 21:12–13; Mark 11:15–17; Luke 19:45–46). Allen D. Callahan suggests in "The Gospel of John" (*True to Our Native Land*, 2007, 188), that the 2:17 reference to Jesus having "zeal" for God's house was added by a later scribe as "spin control on [the] report that Jesus was armed and dangerous [and had] assaulted worshippers and livestock alike."

[65] "Happy festival" or the Hebrew equivalent of "Happy holiday."

there was nothing to see. As soldiers escorted the rabbi away, I followed behind them.

It was never my intent to go beyond the city gate, but by accident or unconscious will, I became part of a crowd of people who followed the soldiers all the way to the outskirts of the city, where they released the rabbi unharmed, and I was amazed because they did so.

I tried blending in and keeping a respectful distance at first. When the others stopped to rest, I stopped, and when everyone stood to continue walking, so did I. And as Jerusalem fell further and further behind me, the less concern I felt about what I was leaving behind, knowing my father had many sons to choose from who could—and would—replace me. With each passing mile, the burdens I had been carrying inside for so long seemed to lighten with each step I took, and I began to feel freer, completely unaware of what following the rabbi would ultimately cost me.

Bit by bit I made my way through the crowd until I was walking directly behind the rabbi, where I instinctively adjusted my stride to match his. I was concentrating so hard on following the pace of his footsteps that when he stopped mid-step and turned to face me, I was unprepared, and walked right into him. "Why are you following me?" he asked. Not in a rude or unkind way but straightforwardly, as though he was curious to know.

The precise answer I gave I cannot recall, but I do remember describing to him the most amazing sight I had ever seen. A rabbi sitting in the square of the temple making a whip, who used it not to harm or injure but to disrupt, oppose and defy, rather than accommodate. "And you lived to tell about it," I said. He stared at me as though searching my very soul, and then he turned around and walked away without saying another word, so I kept walking too.

I was not certain then, and I cannot be completely certain even now, but I do believe that as he was turning around I saw the faintest edge of a smile on the rabbi's face.

That was the day the rabbi became my Teacher, and I began following Him wherever He went, and wherever He went trouble followed like a shadow.

## After the Encounter

For three years, a multitude of people followed my Teacher.

I was with Him, and stayed with Him, because He was what I wanted to be but was not. My plan had been to learn from the Rabbi and then find a place to use whatever gifts I had for GOD's glory, but GOD's plan was that I—and my gifts—were for a time and place of GOD's choosing.[66]

Some people trailed the Teacher after witnessing what He had done with the whip in the marketplace, as I had. Others became part of His following because they were present when He raised His friend Lazarus from the grave, or because they had seen Him do something equally unbelievable. Some made a show of introducing themselves to Him using flattery, hoping to curry favor—growing up I had seen it done many times—but the Rabbi was a very discerning Man with an instinctive ability to recognize the difference between sincere speech and the gift of gab that promises everything and delivers nothing. To such people He gave little attention.[67]

The Rabbi was also a reliable source of food, which attracted a number of other people, and among His followers were those healed by Him of diseases and other ailments. From time to time, He would invite a person to travel with Him, which some declined to do for reasons known only to Himself, and sometimes He denied someone's request to follow Him. Instead, the Rabbi would send the person on their way with a charge to tell others what He had done for them. What I never imagined

---

[66] The image is drawn from Esther 4:14b and Psalm 32:8.
[67] John 2:23–25, 12:17–18.

or considered was the presence of so many women or that they would become the Rabbi's most faithful followers, or that they would take it upon themselves to provide for His needs from their own personal resources. Mary Magdalene was the woman He loved most—who was the closest to Him—but near the end of my Teacher's life, this multitude of people had dwindled to a small crowd, which got smaller and smaller the closer He got to the cross.[68]

From time to time, the Rabbi would go off accompanied by two or three disciples,[69] but I was never one of them, so you may be able to understand the depth of my joy the day He asked me—alone—to go with Him up a mountain. Halfway to the top, the Teacher stopped and gave me instructions to wait there and keep watch until He returned. When He reappeared, I received a message to take to the other disciples who were waiting in our camp below. I made my way back down to them, called out the list of names on my list, evaded questions I was not to answer, and led the chosen individuals back to where the Teacher was waiting. My decision to follow His instructions word for word was unyielding because of a story my mother told me when I was a young boy.

A man sent to the city of Bethel with a message from GOD was directed to go straight to Bethel, deliver the message from the Lord, return by way of a different route, and he was not to stop to eat or drink anything until he was back home. The man went straight to Bethel, delivered the message, and then headed home by a different route. The

---

[68] Matthew 19:2, 27:55–56; Luke 8:1–3, 18:22–23; Mark 5:18–19; John 6:26, 66.
[69] Matthew 17:1; Mark 9:2a; Luke 9:28.

man's troubles began, my mother said, when he ran into an old prophet, whether old in age or usefulness I do not know. The old prophet convinced the man of GOD to go home with him, and the man of GOD ate and drank at the old prophet's table and never made it back home again. As he was killed by a lion soon after leaving, and buried in a grave belonging to the old prophet.[70] That story kept me pretty much on the straight and narrow path, but the lesson that stayed with me is how one decision can change a person's entire life—for good, bad, better or worse.

After arriving at the top of the mountain where the Teacher was waiting for us, we were divided into two groups, one consisting of twelve men and the other consisting of twelve women.[71] After speaking privately with Mary Magdalene, the Rabbi instructed us on living with purpose, direction and without judgment. When the hour grew late, He led us back down the mountain to rejoin the others—but only one of the twenty-four would be at the Teacher's side when He was crucified.

---

[70] 1 Kings 13:1-30a.
[71] Mark 3:13; Luke 6:12. No specific text mentions twelve women, but Mark 3:13 provides room to include more than the traditional twelve male disciples.

Twelve of the Twenty-four

Seeing something from a distance makes a difference in how people see that something, and from a distance what other people saw were twelve harmonious men who called one another brother, but up close our differences and rivalries were on full display.

Two sets of birth brothers overshadowed our little group. The sons of Zebedee, brothers James and John, who were so loud and hot-tempered the Teacher named them Sons of Thunder,[72] and brothers Andrew and Simon, sons of John, who left fishing to answer his call as John the evangelist. All four men were experienced fishers, and they kept us entertained telling tales about their many years working side by side together. Until the four became three, when Andrew left to follow his father.[73]

Shortly after meeting Simon, the Teacher changed his name to Cephas,[74] something Simon was quite proud of and made certain to tell others. I think he interpreted his name change as a badge of honor, a sign the Teacher was holding him up as a model of steadfastness and dependability, having the strength of a rock. As I grew to know Simon better, I came to believe that his renaming had something to do with the

---

[72] Mark 3:17.
[73] Matthew 4:18-21 and Mark 1:16-20 essentially tell the same story. In Luke 5:1-11, Simon is working on the boat alone, his father and Andrew are absent. John 1:40-42 reconnects Andrew with John. In Matthew 16:17, Jesus calls Simon "Bar-Jonah (son or Jonah, or John). *Yochanan* is the Hebrew version of John.
[74] John 1:42. Cephas is a derivative of the Aramaic word *kephas*, meaning rock or stone. Peter derives from the Greek variation of *Petros*, translated to stone or rock.

state of his heart, no less than I still suspect he was somehow involved in the theft for which I was accused.

To be fair, there *were* two Simons in the group, and renaming one did prevent the confusion that would arise from two men responding to the same name. Then again, we also had two men named James and two men named Judas among us, and none of our names changed.

The second Simon was from Cana in Galilee. He met the Rabbi while serving as a freedom fighter in the underground resistance movement against Rome. Simon's commitment to Jewish liberty ran so deep we called him Zealot,[75] instead of by his given name. Not only had he refused to call any man lord—including Caesar and in defiance of Caesar's law—he had been willing and ready to suffer any kind of death for his refusal to do so. Refusing to back down even when his family and friends faced torture and death,[76] until the Teacher came along and convinced him there was a better way.

Levi and his brother James—the other James—were sons of Alphaeus, and the third set of blood brothers in the group.[77] James was a servile and gentle man whose face lit up with adoration every time the Teacher opened His mouth to speak. For a time, I thought James was shy because he never spoke, until I realized one day that he could not speak, except with his hands and eyes, although he could hear as well as any of us. Levi had earned his living collecting taxes for the Roman government, which knew him only as Matthew.[78] Levi told us the job

---

[75] Luke 6:15.
[76] William Whiston, *Josephus, trans., The Complete Works*, Book 18, (Nashville: Thomas Nelson Publishers, 1998), 571, 573.
[77] Mark 2:14, 3:18.
[78] Matthew 9:9, 10:3; Luke 5:27.

paid good money, enough to cover his needs and those of his family, but his work set at odds with the Zealot, who accused him of being a traitor who had unlocked the door for the enemy from the inside. I confess that I, too, wondered at times whether Levi had ever collected more money from the poor than was due and padded his own pocket with the difference, as so many tax collectors did.[79]

The other Judas in the group was Levi's nephew, son of his brother James.[80] Judas was the one everyone depended on to speak what the rest of us were thinking, but were unwilling or too afraid to say.

Philip was a straightforward man with the mind of a bookkeeper. He viewed life through the lens of logic and ledgers and used reason and strategy to think his way through any problem, including seemingly impossible ones.[81]

Nathanael was also from Cana, and he was an honest and plainspoken man with a childlike spirit.[82] By which I mean he never intentionally tried to be clever or polite.

---

[79] Under the Roman system, a tax collector would have paid all the taxes to Rome in advance and then collected the money from citizens and travelers to reimburse himself. Tax collectors who over collected were not generally challenged by taxpayers—at least not successfully—because collection decisions were enforced by Roman soldiers.
[80] Luke 6:16.
[81] John 6:5–7.
[82] John 1:47. Some scholars have suggested that the Bartholomew mentioned in Acts 1:13 is an identifying second name for Nathanael, much like a middle name.

Thomas doubted everything he could not understand. If he could not see, hear, taste, smell or touch something, it just did not exist.[83]

Then there was me, the only Judean among a group of Galilean men who shared hometowns and family ties,[84] the outsider. The other men all spoke with a heavy, very peculiar accent that immediately identified them as Galileans, while my manner of speaking enabled me to pass[85] as though I might be from any number of places within Israel, not to mention I was from a different social class. In the beginning, I think the brothers regarded me as pretentious, just as I regarded them as uncultured and backward, because I had learned growing up that Galilean people were uneducated and simple-minded peasants.

However, I was as wrong about them as they were wrong about me. I was actually in the company of a group of well-informed men who, just like me, shared a love and reverence for GOD and the Torah, and my Galilean Teacher was unlike any rabbi I had ever known. He not just taught *about* GOD, He spoke as though He knew GOD up close and

---

[83] John 11:16, 20:24–25, 21:2. Thomas is a transliteration of the Aramaic word for "twin," but no dependable information exists on who his twin might have been. Bible sources also reference him as "Didymus" (a Greek translation of "Thomas"), such as the New King James Version.

[84] J. Ellsworth Kalas, *The Thirteen Apostles* (Nashville: Abingdon Press, 2002), 95. Operating on the work of others, Kalas suggests "Judas came from Kerioth in Judea . . . all the others being Galileans."

[85] See Mark 14:70 for an example of Galilean speech recognition. In Esther 2:5–11 (especially v. 10), she 'passes' as a Mede or Persian, as instructed by her uncle Mordecai. Allyson Hobbs (*A Chosen Exile: A History of Racial Passing in American Life*) says that for Blacks who look White, passing is a way to offer opportunities that a child would not have living as a Black person. To do so requires that other people be willing to keep the secret, and requires a community to be willing to let the child go and pretend not to know them, even when it hurts.

personal, making rabbinical interpretations with the skill of a much older man and using riddles and parables as GOD had.[86]

Sometimes the other brothers treated me as though I did not quite belong, but never my Galilean Teacher, he always treated me exactly as He did the others. I loved Him for that, and it is a very strange feeling to say that I love a Man in such a tender way, but between me and the other brothers there was—or I felt there was—an emotional distance. Except for the time ten of us stood together in opposition to brothers James' and John's attempt to gain an unfair advantage.[87]

The theft of the money was only one reason for the emotional distance.

---

[86] Ezekiel 17:1–2; Matthew 13:10, 34: Mark 4:2, 10.
[87] Mark 10:35–41; Matthew 20:20–24.

## The Theft

Even now, I do not understand how—no, why—I became keeper of the moneybag.[88]

Levi seemed to me to be a far more logical choice, given his background handling money, or even Philip, but for some reason James, John and Cephas kept urging me to keep the bag. I resisted at first, but when the other brothers began pressing me to take on the responsibility I finally agreed to do it, thinking at the time they were choosing me because they believed I could be trusted to do the job well. I said yes because I knew I could, and would, do a good job.

Cephas donated a small brown leather pouch to the cause, which is where I stored the money we collected, much of which came from the women's efforts. This money is what we used to pay for things like food, taxes and other necessities,[89] as the Teacher directed. To keep the bag secure I kept it tied around my waist at all times, except when bathing in the river.

My accounting routine was always the same. Each evening in the presence of two witnesses, usually Philip and Nathanael, I would total the cost of any purchases made that day. The two witnesses would subtract that amount from the known ending balance of the previous day then count the money in the bag. Day after day, the numbers matched perfectly, until a count one evening revealed that some coins were missing. I never found out who took the coins, but the theft happened

---

[88] John 12:6, 13:29.
[89] Matthew 17:24–25, 22:19a; John 4:8.

early in the day. I left the moneybag hidden under my clothes on the riverbank while I was bathing, as I always did.

My first thought was that a stranger had seen me place the bag under my clothes, waited until I was distracted in the water and then stolen the coins, but the question refusing to be still was why the thief had not taken all the money.

I want to clearly state for the record that none of the brothers ever accused me to my face of stealing, and each one said he was certain the thief had been someone from the outside, but none of them ever spoke in a way that fortified me. I have no evidence pointing to who the actual thief was, and other than my word, I have no evidence proving beyond a doubt that it was not me. The only thing I can say is that my legacy as a thief took root because some unknown, deceitful and unrepentant person said I was one, and other people believed the lie.[90]

After the theft, I kept the money bag tied to my body at all times, even while I was bathing, and I worked even harder to keep my distance from the others, until the day the Teacher chastised me for doing so. He walked up to me, put both His hands on my shoulders, looked me in the eye and said, "The enlightened cannot continue in darkness. Forgiveness is no different from salvation. Trust all things to work together for your good, and think instead about the good things to come."

He patted my shoulders, smiled and walked away.

---

[90] John 12:6.

The Practice Test

Two weeks later, the Teacher sent us out to put our ministry training into practice, without the presence of our Teacher.[91] The thought of this had never occurred to me before that moment, but only because I did not yet understand the relationship between a test and my testimony.

After summoning the twelve of us together, the Teacher instructed us to pair ourselves into six groups of two.[92] James selected John as his partner, Cephas went to stand by Andrew and those of us who remained sorted ourselves according to likability and friendships. Except for the Zealot and me, we became a team by default because we were the last two men standing. We formed a circle around the Teacher and joined hands, He prayed over us and then we received our instructions.

We were never to travel alone but only in the company of our brother-partner, and we were to go only into Jewish towns and villages. We could carry nothing with us—no food, or money, or overnight bag, no staff for the road—and we could wear only one of our two tunics,[93] but that was only the beginning of what the Teacher had to say to us.

"When you enter a town or village," He said, "ask around until you find someone trustworthy to stay with, and remain there for as long as you are in that place. When you enter a home, warmly bless and greet all who live there. When the time comes for you to leave and go on to the

---

[91] The image reminds me of the Civil Rights trainers sending the trainees out to face police, water hoses and attack dogs.
[92] Mark 6:7.
[93] Matthew 10:1, 5–6, 9–10; Mark 6:7–9; Luke 9:1, 3.

next place, and if they have treated you with hospitality, let your blessing remain. If not, take the blessing with you when you leave, and keep it for yourself. If they run you out of town or refuse to listen to you, leave them to themselves, and shake the dust off your feet as you go. Just keep it moving. You will be fed and sheltered by those who receive and welcome you, and I assure you that Sodom and Gomorrah,[94] with all their inhospitable behavior, will be better off on judgment day than those who are inhospitable or unwelcoming to you!"[95]

Our Rabbi struggled to say what He said next.

"I'm sending you out in a defenseless state to travel on dangerous roads, like helpless sheep walking among wolves, but what that means is you will need to be as street smart as a snake and light-footed as a dove. Watch, listen, and be ready to leave at a moment's notice. Travel only with your brother-partner and draw as little attention to yourselves as possible as you go about your business. What you know has been done to me prepare yourselves to receive the same, because a disciple is not above the teacher.

"If the worst thing someone can do to you is kill your body, do not be afraid of them. Do not be afraid of what other people *might* do to you, because in due time everything they have ever done and are doing in

---

[94] Genesis 18:20–21 (Genesis 18:22—19:29).

[95] Matthew 10:13–15. Joseph Telushkin writes in *Jewish Literacy* (p. 588), "In Jewish Law, hospitality (Hebrew, *Hakhnasat Orkhim*) is not just a pleasant social nicety but a serious legal obligation. Inhospitality was viewed not simply as ungracious behavior, but as vile and forbidden." Inhospitality against disciples of Jesus reaches the level of a crime against humanity. See also Acts 13:51 (44-52).

darkness will be revealed. Fear and be in awe only of GOD, who has the power to do away with both your body and soul."[96]

The Rabbi lowered and then lifted His head.

"I intend to leave my peace in this world as a gift to those who belong to me and to my Father in heaven, but each of you needs to understand that I was not sent to bring peace to the Earth. I came carrying a sword in my hand,[97] and with the tip of that sword, I have drawn a line in the sand. On one side is where I stand with my Father, along with all of heaven's hosts and all the souls who have chosen, and will choose, to take their stand with us. On the other side of the line is everyone and everything else. Your duty is to share with others the good news about GOD's gift of forgiveness and salvation, in my name, and extend to them an invitation to come and dine and live with us.[98]

"Those who prefer not to have anything to do with you, or with me, are free to remain where and as they are, but you are to make certain they understand the risks of remaining apart from me.

"I will look away from anyone who looks away from me, and I will deny in the presence of my Father in heaven anyone who denies me in the company of other people. Those who love their family more than me or who decide to turn back when their own cross becomes too heavy to bear, are of no use to me, but hear me also when I say that anyone you meet along the way who welcomes you is, in truth, welcoming me! So,

―――――――――――――――――――

[96] Matthew 10:28; Luke 12:4–5.
[97] Matthew 10:34.
[98] Matthew 22:1-10; Revelation 3:20, 19:9.

tell them for me that because they welcomed me, I will welcome them into the heavenly kingdom where they will receive a reward from the One who sent me, according to the measure of their hospitality. Try your best to help everyone to see that living apart from me will end with them having no life at all, knowing your task will not be an easy one."[99]

At the Teacher's command, we began to disrobe. I took off one sandal, then the other and placed them side by side on the ground. I slipped my outer tunic over my head, folded it neatly and placed it on top of my sandals, then laid my walking stick across my clothes. I remember feeling almost naked. The Teacher gave us the time and place when and where to return and sent us on our way. When I glanced back as the Zealot and I were walking away together, I saw Him gathering our possessions.

30 days later we returned worn and weary, but in good spirits. The Zealot's zeal coupled with my rational-thinking mind made us a good team, and everything the Teacher told us to expect we received and experienced. The hardest part was having to depend on the kindness of strangers for what we needed—food, shelter, everything—but seeing the joy on someone's face who believed the message we shared more than made up for the inhospitable moments we endured.

There was visible relief on the Teacher's face when we all arrived back safely, on time and at the appointed place. Tired as we were, we were also spilling over with tales to tell, and He listened until our exhaustion became as visible to Him as His relief had been to us. The plan was that we would travel to an out of the way resting place in

---

[99] Matthew 10:32–34.

Bethany, but before we could reach the city, a crowd found the Rabbi. Hours later, we were begging Him to send the people home so that they—and we—could eat and rest, but He put us to work feeding them instead, and when we complained about how tired we were, He shut us down. "If you would rather stay in bed," He said, "I would say there's no point in asking GOD to increase your territory."[100]

Not long after, seventy-two more disciples received the same instructions the Teacher had given to us, the exception being they were not to stop and make small talk on the road. Then, He sent them out in pairs of two, as He had done to us. When they all returned alive and well, the Teacher was so happy He danced all around us in a way I imagine king David must have danced in his joy. As though no one was watching.[101]

It pains me to say this, but that moment was only one of two moments that I saw and heard the Rabbi laugh and play like that.

His joy, like His life, was short-lived.

What I admired most was that each time, He held onto the joy of that moments as long as He could.

---

[100] Mark 6:30–32 (30–44); 1 Chronicles 4:10.
[101] Luke 10:1,17 (1–20); 2 Samuel 6:14a.

Just Before the End

The end came not all at once, but after four separate events that happened over the course of several months, beginning with a trip to the Teacher's hometown, His first visit back to Nazareth in a very long while.

As was the custom for visiting rabbis, the Teacher received an invitation to teach in the synagogue. On that Shabbat, He read a passage from the Book of Isaiah, then rolled up the scroll and handed it back to the attendant, and sat down to preach on the text. Every eye was on Him as He confidently and masterfully weaved together a parable contrasting the old law with the new freedom GOD was now offering. He ended with the words, "Today, this scripture has been fulfilled in your hearing."[102]

I will never forget what happened after.

Some people in the synagogue sat whispering and moaning to themselves as they lifted their hands into the air, like children waiting to be lifted-up into loving arms, but others refused to see or accept the Teacher as the promised Messiah sent by GOD. They saw only see the young boy He used to be, saying to one another, "Is this not the son of Mary and Joseph the carpenter?" and "What right does He have to preach to us?"[103]

When the Rabbi made known to them that GOD cared as deeply for Gentiles as GOD cared for Jews, their teeth were completely set on

---

[102] Luke 4:21.
[103] Matthew 13:53-58; Mark 6:1-6; Luke 4:1-29.

edge. When He said that, they dragged Him out of the synagogue and tried to throw Him over a cliff, but with GOD's help moving through individuals, He managed to escape unharmed.[104]

The Teacher never returned to Nazareth after that, but He also never stopped praying for the people who lived there. I know this only because I overheard Him praying on their behalf one evening, and I was listening only because I wanted to know what His prayers sounded like. Most of the brothers, including me, struggled with prayer, to the point Andrew was appointed to go on our behalf and ask the Teacher to teach us how to pray.[105]

The second event leading to the end was King Herod's execution of Rabbi Yochanan,[106] the Teacher's cousin,[107] and father of Andrew and Cephas.[108] When the brothers heard the news, they clung to each other and cried. When the Teacher heard it, He stood very still for several moments as tears rolled down His face, then He was gone, and He stayed away for many days. Not even Mary Magdalene knew where He was. When He returned, it was in the dead of night while everyone was sleeping, but He woke me, motioned for me to remain quiet, and led me out into the desert.

The desert is where the Teacher sometimes went for solitude and prayer, so at the time, I thought that He was taking me with Him for

---

[104] Luke 4:30. Matthew and Mark have different endings.

[105] Luke 11:1.

[106] Matthew 14:3–12; Mark 6:21–28; Luke 9:9a.

[107] Cousins through their mothers, Mary and Elizabeth (Luke 1:39–40, 56), although the exact cousin degree (first, second, third, etc.) is not specified in the Bible.

[108] John 1:40–42. Scholars will say I have taken liberties with the interpretation that John (Yochanan) mentioned in 1:19 and 1:42 are one and the same, and they would be correct.

prayer, as He had taken me alone up the mountain that day. Instead, He took to a small community of people who lived deep in the desert and claimed my Rabbi as their own, calling Him their Teacher of Righteousness. They had made their home in the wilderness so that they could worship and serve GOD free from the demands of the Temple. Everyone had a space to call home, sometimes exchanged as the number of a family's members rose or fell, and everyone in the community shared the responsibility of working and leadership, even children and the elderly had a role to play in the running of the community. No one lacked any essential thing—each need filled by those who had the means to fill it—and playtime was rigidly enforced.[109] It was clear to me that the members of this small community loved my Teacher as much as He clearly loved them.

After His execution, I understood why the Rabbi had taken me there. He was showing and giving me an alternative.

---

[109] George W. Buchanan, "The Priestly Teacher of Righteousness," *Revue De Qumran* 6, no. 4 (24) (1969): 553–558. (It is not difficult to imagine this community as the angels who ministered to Jesus in the wilderness, mentioned in Matthew 4:1 and Mark 1:13. The description of this community also calls to mind Acts 2:42-47).

Calling Out the Temple

The third event happened when the Teacher threw caution to the wind in His handling of the religious leaders who wanted Him dead and out of the way. He stopped engaging them in conversation and began shutting them down in public, one day saying to them, "You're wrong, so stop talking!" and the crowd listening went wild.

Two days later, we were again in the public square when the Teacher's adversaries[110] challenged Him about a point in the Law. He took His time responding, and no one could find fault with His answer, but when He turned the table and posed a question to the religious leaders, not one of them had an answer to give.[111] The look on the His face that day was the same look I had seen in Herod's marketplace, but instead of wielding a whip He lashed out with His tongue. Moving to stand as close as possible to the crowd, Rabbi Yeshua began speaking without restraint.

"I'm talking to my disciples and the people of GOD right now when I say watch out for religious leaders who act pious, and you know the ones I'm talking about! They like to stand out dressed in holy clothes, and referred to by their title in the presence of other people! They expect—even take—the best seats in whatever house they happen to be in, and like to sit in the place of honor at every meal! You know who they are, because you have seen them taking advantage of defenseless widows and lost souls, and heard them reciting long prayers in public to

---

[110] Burse, Cynthia F., *A Little Bible Dictionary*, (Self-published for personal use and distribution, 2022), see *Adversary*. Defined as "One who clearly opposes another; 2. One who outwardly offers or states support for a goal while holding personal views and agendas in direct opposition to that goal."
[111] Matthew 22:41–46.

impress you! So-called leaders who think nothing of putting expectations and extra burdens on *your* backs, but will not do a thing to help you carry the load!

"People, listen carefully to what I'm about to say! Your religious leaders have authority to grant judgments and make decisions—about this, there is no question—they are trained and qualified to tell you what GOD's Law says. So, when they tell you *what* the Law of GOD says to do, do that, but do not do the things you see them doing, because too often there is a world of difference between what they tell you to do and what you see them doing! Remember that pious religious leaders are interested in one thing above all else—playing the part of looking religious! So, watch out for them![112]

"To my disciples I say, don't let anyone call you rabbi, because you have only one Teacher—me—and under no circumstances are you to call any man on Earth father, because you have only one Father, who is in heaven! Your relationship to one another is that of sisters and brothers in service to GOD, and I will say one final time what I have told all of you often enough before. The one who goes about bragging about being somebody important *will be brought low*, but those who humble themselves will be lifted and exalted!"[113]

The Rabbi then turned to face the religious leaders who had banded together along the edge of the crowd.

---

[112] Matthew 23:1–7; Mark 12:38; Luke 20:45–47.
[113] Matthew 23:8–12; Mark 10:31.

"Woe[114] to you hypocritical religious leaders acting so religious as you stand before the people of GOD like a checkpoint blocking the road to heaven! Heaven is *right there* on the other side—right within their reach—but not only do you keep yourselves on the outside, you bear responsibility for denying entry to some and leading others astray! You will travel halfway around the world to find and convert one single soul into accepting your religious beliefs, and when they embrace those beliefs as their own, you make them more of a child of hell than you are![115]

"Woe to you blind guides and hypocrites! You teach people that making a promise with their fingers crossed means nothing, but laying a hand on the Torah[116] and swearing means something! Here, then, is my question to you. Why is the skin on a scroll more meaningful than the skin on a person's hands? You teach people that shaking hands on a promise means nothing, but raising a hand and swearing GOD as your witness does mean something,[117] but here is what I have to say. It does not matter if you shake hands or raise your hand, or if you are inside

---

[114] Horst Balz and Gerhard Schneider, eds., *Exegetical Dictionary of the New Testament*, Volume 2 (Grand Rapids: Eerdmans, 2000), 540. "'Woe' is a cry of regret and pity (or an apocalyptic cry of lament) that when spoken by Jesus "convey[s] the threat of judgment and exclusion from eschatological [divine] salvation."

[115] Matthew 23:13–15, *The Message* (edited).

[116] Christians should feel free to replace the word "Torah" with "Bible."

[117] The Greek religion historian Walter Burkert once said that while "an agreement can be expressed quickly and clearly in words [the agreement] is made effective only by a ritual gesture of some kind." He described the gesture as like "open, weaponless hands stretched out toward one another...grasping in a mutual handshake." One of the earliest known references to the handshake is in a ninth-century B.C. relief showing the Assyrian King Shalmaneser III shaking hands with a Babylonian ruler to seal an alliance.

or outside a house of worship when you make that promise. A promise is a promise, GOD is your witness, and people will be accountable for keeping their promises, no matter how or where they make them![118]

"Woe to you sightless religious hypocrites! You go out of your way to ensure that everything you touch is tithed—every penny of every dollar down to the smallest herb growing in your garden—yet you repeatedly fail to carry out the most important matter of the law, seeing to it that people are treated fairly and with compassion so they can serve GOD! You have been so obsessed with keeping the details of the law that you have lost sight of the law's intent! You make certain your sacramental cups and plates are so clean on the outside they sparkle in the sunlight, but on the inside are full of greed and immorality! In the same way, you religious hypocrites appear righteous on the outside, but inside you are full of lip service, double standards and corruption, like a clean white grave full of dead bones!

"Here, then, is my advice to you. If you want GOD to look on you as clean, get clean on the inside first—*then* attend to everything you touch on the outside![119]

"You build special tombs and monuments to honor the prophets and righteous saints, then have the nerve to say that had *you* lived in their day you would *never* have joined your ancestors as they killed and murdered the prophets! By your own words, then, you admit to being the children of those who murdered them, and because of people like you, GOD had to *keep* sending prophets, wise guides and scholars— one right after the other, generation after generation—and each time you

---

[118] Matthew 23:13–22, *The Message* (edited).
[119] Matthew 23:23–31, revised from *The Message*.

and your ancestors abused and treated them like dirt and hunted them down with lynch mobs! You and your ancestors are why every single drop of righteous blood ever spilled on this Earth—from the blood of innocent Abel to the blood of Zechariah, whom you secretly murdered between the sanctuary and the altar—will come down on the heads of *this* generation! It is time, now, for you to finish what your ancestors started." [120]

The Rabbi took one long, last look across the sea of people and at the agitated religious leaders, then turned and walked away.

From that day on, no one dared publicly question Him about anything, [121] and He kept to himself, surrounded only by family and those He considered friends.

The fourth and final thing happened just before the end.

---

[120] Genesis 4:1–8; Matthew 23:29–36. Perhaps "from Abel to Zechariah" is a figurative or metaphorical expression similar to "from A to Z and everything in between." The themes present in these "Woes" call to mind the Parable of the Tenant in Matthew 21:33-41 and Luke 20:9-16.
[121] Matthew 22:46.

Outside the Gates of Jerusalem

As we traveled to Jerusalem for what would be our last Passover together, the Teacher stopped about twelve miles outside the city gates so that everyone could rest. After taking His turn for water, He went and sat by Himself. I sat with the others, staring at His back and half listening to the festive Passover talk going on around me.

Many times, Rabbi Yeshua had told us what was going to happen to Him one day in Jerusalem.[122] Including the details of how, where and who would kill Him, but we never talked about the matter among ourselves. Nor do I believe any of us ever really believed it would happen—until it did. I think we all thought that by not talking about what was to come, we could somehow keep it from happening, and even as the Teacher sat alone with His back facing us, none of us reached out to Him.

The thought running through my mind that day was that someone needed to say something to Him—to be with Him—but it was also difficult to believe He was in any real mortal danger, because everyone else was acting within their range of normalcy.

Mary could reach Him in ways no one else could, but she and another disciple were away on an errand.[123] I finally got up the nerve to go and sit beside my Teacher, but I did not speak. When He did not ask me to leave I was certain He needed a friend, and I thought long and hard about what to say, knowing it had to be something that would encourage

---

[122] Matthew 16:21, 17:22-23, 20:18-19, 21:1-3; Mark 8:31-32a, 9:31, 10:33; Luke 9:21-22, 31-33, 44; John 6:66.
[123] Matthew 21:1-2; Mark 11:1-2; Luke 19:28-30.

Him and lift His spirits. Especially because so many others had given up on Him, and left Him.

I leaned my head toward His and said, "I know who You are and from what place You have come. You have come from the immortal world, and I am not worthy to pronounce the name of the One who sent You," but the Rabbi did not move or react in any way.

Until He closed His eyes, lowered His head and said, "Move away from the others, and I will explain the mysteries of the kingdom to you. Not to ensure that you make it there, but to prepare you for the deep grief you are about to experience, because someone is going to take your place."[124]

My heart was pounding so hard I thought it would come out of my chest, and my mouth was so dry I could not swallow. I got up and walked to stand beneath a nearby tree, hoping it was far enough away for privacy but close enough for the Teacher to see where I had gone. My mind was racing, along with my heart, because I could not understand

―――――――――――――――――

[124] Marvin Meyer, ed. and trans., *The Nag Hammadi Scriptures: The Revised and Updated Translation of Sacred Gnostic Texts* (New York: HarperCollins, 2007), 761. The image for me created by the phrase "someone is going to take your place" is that of a relay runner having the baton snatched out of their hand as another takes their place as lead person for the team. The reported name of the man who replaced Judas was Matthias (Acts 1:12:26 (12–26), and like Barnabas, his true contribution to Jesus' ministry is unknown. It seems reasonable to conclude that Matthias was a known entity to the other disciples, because I cannot imagine that such an important ministry position would be filled with someone who had not already demonstrated faithful belief in Jesus. Too much was at stake.

why someone was going to take my place, or what I had done to cause such a terrible thing to happen.

When the Rabbi joined me on the large stone where I was sitting, so that we sat facing one another, He began explaining GOD's kingdom to me, and my place in it and what it was He needed me to do. I was to go to the Jewish high priest and convince him of my willingness to hand the Teacher over to the Jewish Council in exchange for money.[125] If the priest agreed, at the appointed time I was to lead the Teacher's adversaries to our regular meeting place in the garden. When I saw the Teacher, I was to follow His lead. When the time came to engage His plan, He would give me a sign. I was to tell no one what I was doing, and the other details of the plan He would leave for me to arrange.

For the first time, I walked away from my Teacher.

I understood immediately why my place among the twelve would be lost, and why grief would become my constant companion.

Who would want anything to do with the man responsible for handing GOD's Savior over to His enemies?

I turned around to ask the Rabbi this very question, but He was already sitting with the other disciples.

---

[125] Matthew 26:14-15; Mark 14:10-11a; Luke 22:4-5.

## The Decision

The Teacher gave me the sign during what would be our last meal together.

Everyone was sitting and waiting for the serving of the meal, when the Rabbi announced that someone sitting around the table would be handing Him over to Jewish authorities. Everyone began asking at the same time, "Is it me, Lord?" but He said, "Saying so doesn't make it so."[126]

I said nothing, but neither did I exclude myself from the question, because I had not yet decided whether I would—or could—do what the Teacher needed done. Then the sign appeared.

He took hold of a piece of bread and said, "The one to hand me over is the one to whom I give this dipped piece of bread."[127] He dipped the bread into a bowl containing His favorite broth and then extended the dripping morsel to me. Two or three drops fell to the table before I reached out my hand to take hold of His offering. He said very softly, "Do it quickly"[128] and released the bread into my hand, which I put into my mouth.

As the Teacher continued to dip and serve pieces of bread to those seated around the table,[129] I tried not to attract attention as I

---

[126] Matthew 26:20-22; John 13:21-22.
[127] John 13:26.
[128] John 13:27.
[129] Matthew 26:26; Mark 14:22; Luke 22:17. The bread in this last supper scene

removed the moneybag from around my waist and placed it under the table, hidden but easy enough to find.

The moment I stood to my feet Cephas shouted, "Judas, where are you going?" but I ignored him and walked out into the night. [130]

---

[130] John 13:21–30 (see also Matthew 26:20–25).

## The Arrest

I kept to the Teacher's plan and led the religious officials and a detachment of Jewish troops to the place in the garden where I knew He would be waiting. Our coming was announced before we actually appeared by a night sky lit by the flaming torches we carried.[131]

When the Rabbi and the other disciples came into view, I immediately stopped walking, halting those with me, and waited for Him to make the next move. My heart was pounding, but I kept my eyes fixed on my Teacher's face. When He saw me standing there a smile came to His lips, and He began walking toward me. I followed His lead and began walking toward Him, until we were holding on to one another in a tight embrace, and I tried without success to hold back my tears. He said "Thank you, my friend," and then released me. I bowed to Him and kissed His hand in devotion, and then moved to stand a short distance away.[132]

When the Jewish officials announced who they were looking for and the Rabbi identified Himself, soldiers immediately surrounded Him, but He did not resist arrest. As two of the officers grabbed His arms, the Teacher asked that His disciples be allowed to go free,[133] and a third soldier responded by kicking His legs out from under Him, so that He fell face down into the dirt. Another soldier put his knee in the bend of the Teacher's back, making it difficult for Him to breathe, as two other soldiers bound His wrists and ankles with shackles and chains.

---

[131] John 18:1-3; Matthew 26:47; Mark 14:43; Luke 22:47a.
[132] Matthew 26:48-50a; Mark 14:44-45; Luke 22:47b-48.
[133] Matthew 26:50b; Mark 14:46; John 18:4-8.

When the other eleven disciples saw the Teacher being taken down in this way, Andrew and the Zealot unsheathed their swords and shouted, "Lord, should we attack?" but Cephas withdrew the sword concealed beneath his coat and immediately lunged toward a man named Malchus, cutting off his right ear. The Teacher shouted, "Put your weapons away! You can't stop this!"[134] His words muffled, because soldiers were pressing His head against the ground. Everyone put their sword back into its sheaths, but panic was on their faces, because no one knew what to do next. Not until the Jewish officials began whispering among themselves and pointing toward them, which is when the disciples ran away into the darkness.[135]

As soldiers were leading the Rabbi away, I walked closely behind and to His right, shortening my steps to match the shuffling gait created by the shackles on His ankles. When I looked behind me a short time later, for no particular reason, I saw that Cephas was secretly following behind us.[136]

---

[134] Matthew 26:51-54; Mark 14:47-51; Luke 22:49-51a; John 18:10-11.
[135] Matthew 26:56b; Mark 14:50 (also see Zechariah 26:58).
[136] Matthew 26:58; Mark 14:54a; Luke 22:54; John 18:15a.

The Trial—Part I

We went first to the home of Annas, the high priest who had given me money to hand the Teacher over. The doorkeeper recognized me from my earlier visits and waved me in. When I realized that Cephas was not in the room, I left the Teacher's side to go and look for him and found him standing outside with some of Annas' servants and soldiers, warming himself by a fire.[137] I spoke with the doorkeeper, and Cephas gained entry into the house. For reasons of his own, he did not stay, nor did I try to stop him from leaving.

When Annas entered the room, he began aggressively interrogating the Teacher about His followers and beliefs, but the Rabbi responded in as calm and collected a manner as I had ever seen. He said, "I've spoken in public on a regular basis where the whole world heard me. I have taught openly in the synagogue—nothing I said is secret—so why are you interrogating me? Why not go out, find some of the people who heard me speak and question them? They can tell you exactly what I've taught."[138]

Straightaway, one of the arresting officers walked over and backhanded the Rabbi on the right side of His face with such force His lip split, and He swayed slightly, but the expression on His face remained calm, majestic and unafraid. He turned and offered His other cheek as well,[139] but His assailant had already turned away and was walking back

---

[137] Matthew 26:69a; Mark 14:66–67; Luke 22:55; John 18:25a.
[138] John 18:19–21.
[139] John 18:22 (Matthew 5:39b; Luke 6:29). In Jewish law, hitting someone's face was a significant act of hostility. The direction of the strike, typically using

to his post. The Rabbi spit out a mouthful of blood and said, "If I've said something that is not true, I would appreciate your pointing out to me what it is I'm lying about. If what I have said is correct, why are you hitting me?" Several hours of interrogation later, still bound by shackles and chains, He was taken to the Sanhedrin Council and handed over to Caiaphas, the legally appointed ruling high priest that year, and son-in-law of Annas.[140]

Even before the trial began—if that is what they intended it to be—the outcome had already been decided. What Caiaphas and the Council members wanted was enough evidence to charge the Teacher with a crime worthy of execution, but no such evidence existed or was forthcoming. A long line of people had volunteered—or been summoned—to testify against Him, yet not one testimony agreed with another. For this reason, I began hoping in my heart He might be released.[141]

But when two men stepped forward to say they both heard the Rabbi say He could tear the Temple down and rebuild it again in three days,[142] twisting His words to make them mean something He never intended, that's when my hope died a thousand deaths, and I knew for certain that nothing could change what was about to happen.

---

the right hand, signified the attacker's intent. A backhand blow was to insult, not injure. In this scene, Jesus demonstrates the meaning of the phrase "turning the other cheek." It is both an act of defiance and a sign that one is self-assured and unafraid.

[140] Matthew 26:57; Luke 22:66; John 11:45-53, 18:23–24.
[141] Matthew 26:59–60a; Mark 14:55–56; John 2:19. Jewish law allowed for the death penalty on the testimony of two consistent witnesses.
[142] Matthew 26:60b; Mark 14:57–59.

The testimony of the two agreeing witnesses transformed Caiaphas into a raging lunatic. He shouted, "What do you have to say in your defense about what these men have said against you?!" but my Teacher said nothing. "Have you no response to these accusations?! What exactly are these two men accusing you of?!" but again, there was no response. Caiaphas was so furious he stood directly in front of the Teacher and shouted at His face, "Tell us plainly, under sacred oath before the living GOD! Are you the Anointed One?! Do you claim to be the Son of GOD?!" [143]

That's when the Teacher lifted His head, looked Caiaphas in the eye and said, "You said that, not me, but even if I said you speak the truth you wouldn't believe me, and if I were to ask you if you yourself believed what you said, you wouldn't answer me. But do believe me when I say that in the not-too-distant future, the next time you see me, I'll be seated on heavenly clouds as the right-hand power of GOD." [144]

Caiaphas turned toward the other Council members, tore his clothes and shouted, "Enough! We have heard enough! There is no further need for witnesses! You heard His blasphemy for yourselves! So, what is your decision? What will your judgment be?!" [145]

---

[143] Matthew 26:62-63; Mark 14:60-61; Luke 22:66b-7a (see also John 11:45-53).
[144] Matthew 26:64; Mark 14:62; Luke 22:67b-69. (See also Matthew 24:29–31; Mark 13:24–27; Luke 21:25–28; Revelation 14:14, 16).
[145] Matthew 26:65–66; Mark 14:63–64a; Luke 22:70–71. In Jewish tradition, the tearing of clothes, or rending of garments, is *kriah*, a Hebrew word meaning tearing. The act symbolizes grief, deep distress, anger, or mourning in one's heart.

The members of the Council spoke as one as they rendered their judgment. Rabbi Yeshua of Nazareth was worthy of death.

They blindfolded Him, and took turns hitting and spitting on Him as they laughed and shouted, "Tell us Prophet, who hit you?!" They were brutal and abusive, saying and doing all manner of profane and irreverent things to Him. [146]

---

[146] Matthew 26:66b–68; Mark 14:64b–65.

## The Trial—Part II

The Council took the Rabbi to the headquarters of Pontius Pilate, the governor of Judea, although Caiaphas and the other members refused to enter the palace, on the grounds that doing so would make them ritually unclean and unfit to eat the Passover meal, forcing Pilate to come out to them. [147] In truth, there was much more to that moment than ritual cleanliness.

Whatever personal agendas and feelings the members of the Sanhedrin Council may have had concerning my Teacher, regarding Pilate they were of one mind. Bad blood had existed between the governor and the Jewish people for some time because of his monstrous behavior. Not only had Pilate ordered his soldiers to rob the Temple treasury to fund the construction of a water pipeline for Rome, he had thousands of Jews massacred when they protested. He refused to listen to any concerns put forth by Jews. For these reasons and more, the Council had written on numerous occasions to Vitellius, Pilate's superior, to complain about him. Their complaints were so frequent that both Pilate and the Council knew another complaint put him at risk of losing his command. Forcing Pilate to come out to him was Caiaphas' way of reminding the governor of who was actually governing the situation. For his part, Pilate knew he could not risk releasing an unexamined man accused of treason and sedition.

Soldiers forced me into the crowd, separating me from the Rabbi, and I blended in as only one of many witnesses watching a tragedy unfold before our eyes.

---

[147] Matthew 27:2; Luke 23:1; John 18:28–29.

Pilate walked over to examine the Teacher, who was staring off at a point somewhere between heaven and the horizon, bruised from the beatings inflicted on Him and filthy from dried spit and blood, dirt and lack of water. Pilate then moved to stand near the edge of the porch where the Sanhedrin members had gathered below the railing. Caiaphas was standing on a platform of some kind that elevated him above the crowd, putting him at eye level with the governor.

Pilate asked, "What charges are you bringing against this man?" and Caiaphas responded for the Council.

"Do you think we would waste our time bringing this man to you if he were not guilty of doing evil things? He claims to be a king!" a charge Caiaphas knew Pilate could not afford to ignore.

The governor went back to the Teacher and asked, "Are you a king?" and He answered, "Your saying so doesn't make it so," and His voice sounded as weary as His battered body looked.

Pilate immediately turned away and walked back to the edge of the porch. "I find no guilt in this man!" he announced, but the Council members would not let the matter go.

They shouted, "He is agitating and provoking the whole of Judea!" and Pilate shouted back, "Then take Him away and judge Him by your own laws!" "Our laws don't permit us to kill anyone!"[148] but Pilate

---

[148] John 18:29–31; Luke 23:3–6.

was already walking back into the building. Two soldiers then grabbed hold of the Teacher and pushed Him inside.

For the record, what Caiaphas said was not true. Had my Teacher been guilty of any of the crimes the Council said He committed, they could have sentenced Him to death in a number of ways. They could have stoned Him, the method of execution Jews seemed to prefer,[149] or they could have had His body burned,[150] which happened mainly among the Gentiles. They could have had Him crushed or strangled to death, but they chose not to any of these things. They chose instead to gamble that facing off against Pilate and making him kill the troublemaking Rabbi would prove to be a more expedient option, and it did. It saved the Council from dealing with a mountain of procedural barriers, put in place to ensure capital punishment was a rare event.

The door to the palace opened and soldiers brought the Teacher out again, but they took Him back inside almost right away. When Pilate came out a short time later he announced his intention to hand the Teacher over to Herod the king, who was in Jerusalem for Passover, because Nazareth was part of Herod's jurisdiction,[151] and it was a clever move on Pilate's part. It took the spotlight off him, giving him time to think of other ways Herod might prove useful. When I later heard the two men had become friends,[152] the news was of no surprise to me, because they were kindred spirits.

---

[149] Exodus 17:4; Leviticus 20:1–2, 24:16, 23; Numbers 14:10a, 15:35–36; 1 Samuel 30:6; John 8:7 (1–11), 10:31; Acts 7:57–59; Hebrews 11:37.
[150] Genesis 38:24; Leviticus 20:14, 21:9; Daniel 3:6, 15b, 24–25 (The concept of being thrown into fire takes on a larger role in apocalyptic thought: i.e., Matthew 13:47–50 and Revelation 20:10).
[151] Luke 23:11 (6–11).
[152] Luke 23:12.

The Council would normally have avoided Herod at all costs, but that day Caiaphas and the others were eager to have an audience with Herod, to present their accusations to him as they had with Pilate, but Herod sent the Teacher back to the governor free of charges or judgments. When they returned to the governor's palace, soldiers took the Rabbi inside, where He remained for some time before they brought Him out again. [153]

Pilate reappeared on the porch and gave his final ruling to the Council. "You presented this Man to me as an insurgent and an agitator, but I have examined Him and find no basis for your accusations! Herod has examined Him as well and found no basis for your accusations! Together, we have determined that this Man has done nothing deserving of the death penalty! You see for yourselves that He has been thoroughly punished, as a warning to others not to disturb the peace, but my final judgment is that this Man is *not* guilty of your accusations and charges and I am going to release Him!" [154]

Pilate turned to go back inside, as though the matter was over and done, but the council members shouted "No! No! No!"

He walked back to the edge of the porch and attempted to speak directly to the people.

"You people have a custom during Passover that would permit me to have mercy and release a prisoner to you! Who do *you* want me to release—Yeshua of Nazareth or Yeshua Barabbas?" and the crowd shouted their answer. "Free Barabbas!"

---

[153] John 18:33–38.
[154] John 18:38b; Luke 23:13–16.

Pilate argued against releasing Barabbas because of his convictions as a murderer and an insurrectionist. When that failed to persuade the people, he tried to reason with them again, but the crowd would not listen. Someone yelled, "Free Barabbas! Free Barabbas! Free Barabbas," and the people took up the chant. "Free Barabbas! Free Barabbas! Free Barabbas!" [155]

Soldiers rushed the Teacher and Pilate inside the palace. When they came out again, there were clear signs the Rabbi had endured another beating. He was wearing a purple robe around His shoulders, pushed down on His head was a twisted crown made of thorny branches, and His face, neck and shredded clothing were drenched in blood.

Pilate stood before the crowd a third time and announced, "I find no fault in this Man!" [156]

Members of the Council began shouting, "Crucify Him! Crucify Him!" and the crowd began shouting with them, "Crucify Him! Crucify Him!" The sound of their voices was so loud, I was certain all of Jerusalem could hear them, which made it impossible to hear what Pilate was trying to say.

Caiaphas raised his hand above his head and the crowd became silent, as though on command.

---

[155] John 18:39-40; Luke 23:18-19 (The earliest manuscripts omit Luke 23:17, and some Bible translations and paraphrases, i.e., the ESV and *The Message*, have continued that tradition); Matthew 27:15–21; Mark 15: 6–11.
[156] John 19:1-5; Luke 23:20-22.

Once more Pilate declared that the Teacher was not guilty of any wrongdoing worthy of capital murder, or of any punishable crime.

The high priest shouted "Crucify Him!" and Pilate shouted back, "*You* take and crucify Him! I've declared Him not guilty of any punishable crime!"[157] Pilate seemed determined not to back down from his decision.

Not until one of the members of the Sanhedrin Council said, "We have a law, and according to our law, this Man should die because He claims to be the Son of GOD!"[158] When Pilate heard the real reason why the Council wanted the Teacher dead, he was terrified.[159]

He walked back over to where the Rabbi was standing, hunched over and weighed down by shackles and chains.

Pilate asked, "Where are you from? What evil have you done?" but the Teacher did not respond. Pilate said, "Don't you know I have the power to save you?"[160] The Teacher said to him, "The only thing you can do to me is what heaven allows you to do. The evil done concerning me belongs not to you, but to those who handed me over to you."[161]

Pilate stared at my Teacher as though he could not believe what he was hearing, before turning back to face the crowd and shout, "I find no guilt in this Man!"

---

[157] John 19:6.
[158] John 19:7.
[159] John 19:8.
[160] John 19:9–10.
[161] John 19:11.

The members of the Council led the crowd to begin chanting again. "Crucify Him! Crucify Him! Crucify Him!" until Caiaphas raised his hand again to silence them and issue a warning to Pilate.

"Anyone who makes himself a king speaks against Caesar, and we have no king *but* Caesar. If you let this man go free, it will prove to everyone—especially to Caesar—that you are *not* Caesar's friend!"[162]

When Pilate heard that, he surrendered to the Council's demand. Barabbas was freed from his prison cell, and my Teacher was handed over to Roman soldiers to be crucified.[163]

---

[162] John 19:12–15.
[163] John 19:16; Luke 23:23–25; Matthew 27:26; Mark 15:15.

### The Conclusion of Judas' Testimony

When I went returned to Annas' house one final time, I found him sitting alone in his inner den. I threw the money he had given me at his feet and walked away.[164]

Later that day, from a distance, I watched as they crucified my Teacher. Then I followed Mary and the others to the place where they buried Him, taking care they did not see me.

I sat high up in the rocks. Hiding and watching until the sun went down and disappeared. Waiting until the only person left at the tomb was Mary Magdalene. When she took her leave, I made my way down the side of the small mountain until I was standing on level ground again.

I took off one sandal, then the other, and placed them side by side on the ground. I removed one of the two tunics I was wearing, folded it neatly, placed it on top of my sandals, and laid my walking stick across my belongings. Carrying no food, no money, no overnight bag, no staff for the road, and wearing only one of my two tunics, I headed into the desert toward the one place I thought might take me in, and I wasn't wrong. I shared all of what had happened, and they found a place for me.

Having faithfully discharged my duties, I wait now for the return of the One to whom all faithfulness is due.

Thank you, Your Honor, for this opportunity to give my testimony.

---

[164] Matthew 27:3–5.

# The Testimony of Mary Magdalene

## The Allegations

*(Mary takes a seat in the chair occupied at one time by Judas Iscariot)*

Court Official: "Please state your name for the record."

    I am Mary of Magdala, daughter of GOD.

Judge: "Mary Magdalene is the name presented in the document before this court. Are you and Mary Magdalene one and the same person? Do you answer to this name as well?"

    The answer to both questions is yes, Your Honor.

Judge: "Thank you for the verification. The understanding of this court is that you wish to offer testimony today regarding allegations of prostitution and demonic possession made against you by the Christian Church. Is the court's understanding correct?"

    It is, Your Honor.

Judge: "Then we can proceed. The court is pleased to be able to provide this opportunity for you to give your testimony. It is also obligated to inform you it has no jurisdiction or authority over the church, nor can this court undo any wrongs that may have been committed against you. However, the church is on the schedule to give testimony in a different court, which does have jurisdiction. Today is for you, so that you can tell your side of the story uninterrupted. Do you understand all that has been said?"

    I understand, Your Honor.

Judge: "Very good. Please proceed when you're ready, and take as much time as you need."

## Mary's Counterstatement

Concerning the church's accusation of demonic possession, I have only this to say.

I have spent the better part of my life reminding people about the destiny of infatuated believers, who Yeshua said are about as helpful as a lamp without oil. I have been a playmate and comrade to those who fear GOD and keep righteous instruction.

I have spoken out in concern and warning to religious people who see nothing wrong with separating words of faith and belief from the practice of faithful behavior. Who say to themselves, "This thing is for GOD, but this other thing is for myself. This matter concerns my soul, but this other matter is for my body's pleasure."[165] Who spend six days out of seven thinking of ways to invoke words of praise from people they admire and envy. Divinely created in the image of GOD, and yet they aspire to nothing greater than becoming the imagined greatness of someone else.

If saying these things are signs of demonic possession, then call me demon possessed, as Yeshua's enemies called Him demon possessed, and called every woman following Him demon possessed.[166] My reality is that GOD is at the center of my thoughts. GOD's Word has given me hope. I take comfort and delight in GOD's righteous commands, which I love and have promised to obey. I believe GOD's promise to grant me

---

[165] This concept is adapted from "Religion" in Kahlil Gibran's *The Prophet* (1923), 77.
[166] Matthew 12:24; Mark 16:9; Luke 8:2–3, 11:15; John 8:48, 10:20.

eternal life, and this knowledge is my comfort during any, and all, affliction.[167]

Regarding the accusation of prostitution, I will say only this.

Of all the women prostitutes I have known and lived with, not one engaged in the practice of servicing men because she enjoyed doing it. Prostitution is a transactional relationship. She gives something of value, and in return, she receives something she needs more. Nor does prostitution make a woman unfit for the heavenly kingdom. Except in the minds of mean-spirited people who give their own opinions more weight and importance than may be good for them, or in the mind of a practicing prostitute who believes in error that she is only what other people have judged her to be.

I have lived long enough to know that prostitution is what happens when a woman reaches a crossroad. She can no longer keep going on the way she has been anymore, because her circumstances have changed and not for the better, forcing her to do something differently and to do it right away. Doing differently is a difficult and frightening thing to do, but going through that difficult time is what leads a woman to become as courageous as Rahab, or as extravagantly unsparing as was the woman with the alabaster jar.[168]

In contrast, men tend to prostitute themselves for personal glory and gain.

---

[167] Psalm 119:43, 47, 50, 55.
[168] Joshua 2:1–21; Matthew 26:6–13; Mark 14:3–9; Luke 7:36–50.

I have nothing more to say about the accusations made against me by the Christian church, but I do have much more to say for the record, to the glory of GOD.

## This little Light of Mine

My mother's parents raised me in Magdala, a little fishing town in the western part of Israel close to the shore of the Galilean Sea,[169] and as far back as I can remember it was always just the three of us.

My mother was an only child who died shortly after giving birth to me, and my father's life ended less than a year later, killed by robbers. Living through the horror of those tragedies must have been terrible for my grandparents, but as a child, I knew only joy.

I was awakened each morning by the sound of my grandfather praying, but what neither of us realized at the time was that waking to words of prayer safeguarded my mind, ensuring my first thought each day was centered on GOD, whose image was being formed morning-by-morning, bit by bit. At night, which was my favorite time of day, my grandfather would read me to sleep with stories from the Torah, and each story ended with the coming of a hero who would rescue GOD's people from all our enemies.

I grew up believing that the words spoken by the rabbi in the synagogue were true. GOD had indeed been present the day my parents conceived me, and knew me better than I knew myself, and had formed the details of my body to be unlike any other, and written a to do list for every day of my life—all before I was even born.[170] As a child, I felt free, as though I had been set loose to run through wheat fields ready for

---

[169] For context, the majority population in the modern western part of Israel is Palestinian.
[170] Psalm 139:13–16.

harvest. That was my state of mind the day I heard the rabbi say, "Delight yourself in the Lord!"[171]

Obediently, I began to delight myself in the Lord with great delight.

Sometimes, for no obvious reason and moving to a tune that only I could hear, I would throw my arms high into the air and whirl and dance around the room until I fell on the floor in exhaustion. Other times, I would beat an empty pot with my hand as I leaped about, pretending to be Mariam with her tambourine.[172] As I was frolicking about in that way one day, my grandmother asked me the name of my dance. "Freedom!" I yelled, and then threw my little arms around her wide hips and hugged her with such zeal she almost fell over.

I looked up at her face, expecting to see a reflection of my own joy, but at the time, I could not tell by her smile if she was saddened or pleased by what I said. Many years passed before I understood that her smile was a pained recognition that the only person in the room who truly believed I was free, was me. Life had not yet taught me about the invisible harness placed around my neck the moment I was born a girl.

Shortly after my fifth birthday, I learned this lesson about life.

The day was warm and bright and began like any other day, except that day I was to accompany my grandmother to the marketplace for the very first time. I was so excited I could barely hold still as she dressed me, until she threatened to leave me at home.

---

[171] Psalm 37:4.
[172] Exodus 15:20.

My feet skipped and hopped to match my grandmother's stride as we walked to the market, and I held tightly to her right hand as my right hand conducted the music playing in my mind. It was a long walk, but at the sight of our destination, all my tiredness went away.

As she weaved in and out among the crowd, I clung tightly to my grandmother's dress, pressing my body against hers. When she stopped to select fresh fruits and vegetables and negotiate with vendors about prices, I watched and listened with the seriousness of a child. As we moved from one stall to the next, she would often stop to talk with other women who, like my grandmother, were dressed in black from head to toe. Completely invisible except for their eyes. I tried to listen to their conversations, but the distance between their mouths and my ears, and the layers of clothing they wore, proved too difficult to overcome. Which freed me to busy myself dancing in circles around them.

The terrible thing happened as we were leaving the marketplace.

Outside the gate, a crowd of people had gathered. Because of my size, it was hard to see what was happening, but when my grandmother moved us closer to the inner part of the circle, I saw men beating another man, as bystanders encircled them and watched. The attackers kept hitting the man's body and face with stones held in their fists, and they did not stop until he was little more than a bloody lump of flesh. For the first time in my life, I felt fear.

I could not understand why no one was helping the man, so I grabbed my grandmother's hands with my own and began pulling her in his direction. I pleaded with her, "We have to help him!" but she grabbed my arm and jerked me back to her side and said, "Hush child!" in a way she had never spoken to me before. It frightened me, so I immediately hushed and stood still. When my grandmother did not attempt to shield my eyes from the violence, I covered them with my own small hands, but my ears had no means by which to protect themselves. It never occurred to me to close my eyes and use my hands to cover my ears.

When the sounds of the beating finally stopped, I lowered my hands from my eyes. The man's face and clothes were drenched in blood, his eyes were swollen shut and he was weaving unsteadily on his feet, until he fell to the ground. One of the attackers walked over to the man's body and spat on him. When he tried to raise himself up from the ground, a different attacker took a stick and kept hitting him until the man's body did not move anymore. As the assailants began walking away, one by one, and even after they were long gone, still no one moved to help the beaten man lying injured in the street.

As my grandmother led me away from that terrible scene on that terrible day, I kept looking back, hoping each time the man would be standing on his feet again. More than once, I thought of snatching my hand away from hers and running back to help him in some way, but I was too afraid to try. When I turned to take one final look, the man was so far away I could barely make him out anymore. I never did learn the reason why the men did what they did, but witnessing their violence put an end to my innocence.

Many years later I told Yeshua about that terrible day, and not long after, He began telling and teaching a story about a man who was beaten by robbers and left for dead.[173]

Before that terrible day, I lived what was an ordinary life in an ordinary family in an ordinary town filled with ordinary people.

---

[173] Luke 10:25-37.

On that terrible day, I saw another person as myself for the first time, my childhood illusions ended, and my little light briefly stopped shining.

Holding Fast to Liberty

After that terrible day, nothing seemed very different. Life resumed the rhythm it had always had. Grandmother took care of the house—and shopped without me—and meals were served at the scheduled times. I still had chores to do, and my grandfather went about his normal rabbinical duties teaching would-be rabbis who constantly trailed behind him. I was what was different.

For several weeks, I had nightmares most every night, sometimes waking in such a disturbed state I could barely be consoled. On one especially bad night, my grandfather responded to my distress. He came to me, scooped me out of my bed and sat me down on his lap to hold me. I threw my arms around his neck and buried my head in his shoulder, squeezing him so tightly I feel certain he could barely breathe, and I cried like a wounded animal. I was still crying when he stood up with me in his arms, carried me over to the corner of the house where he studied and set me down on my own two feet. I stood there crying and wiping away tears, as my grandfather selected a scroll from the collection and unrolled it. He found what he was looking for and said to me, "Come and read this please." I went to stand beside him, wiped the tears from my eyes, fixed my attention on the word beneath the tip of the yad[174] and began to read.

"The Lord…is…my…rock, my for-tress…and my de-liv-er-er."

---

[174] The term *yad* has three different Hebraic meanings, one of which is pointer to indicate the place one is reading from in the Torah.

"De-li-ver-er," Grandfather said. "De-li-ver-er," I repeated. He nodded and gestured for me to continue.

"My GOD…is my rock, in who-m…I take ref-uge…re-fuge…my shi-eld…and the horn…of my…sal-va-tion, my…strong-hold and my re-fuge, my…sav-i-or…"

"Savior," he said.

"Savior," I repeated. "You save me from vi-o-lence."

"Now, read this," he said. My eyes followed the tip of the yad.

"In my dis-tress…I call-ed…called u-pon…up-on the Lord; to my GOD…I called. From…GOD's tem-ple…GOD hear-d…heard my voice, and my cry…came to GOD's ears."[175]

"Read it again," he said, and I read it again. There must have still been some measure of uncertainty in my voice, because my grandfather told me to read it again, and then again. I took a deep breath and read more slowly, as though consuming each word.

"The Lord is my rock…my fortress…and my deliverer;

My GOD…my rock…in whom I take refuge,

My shield…and the horn of my salvation,

My stronghold…and my refuge,

My Savior…You save me from violence.

In my distress…I called to the Lord…to my GOD I called.

---

[175] 2 Samuel 22:2-3, 7 (ESV).

From GOD's temple…GOD heard my voice…and my cry came to GOD's ears."

My grandfather returned the scroll to the cupboard and asked me, "What did you learn?" and I remember the moment like it was yesterday. I said, "I don't have to be afraid, because GOD is strong and will come to my rescue."

He was unconvinced. "Repeat what you said, a little louder this time please."

I raised what I thought was a mighty voice and said, "I don't have to be afraid, because GOD is strong and will come to my rescue!"

Still, he was not satisfied. "I'm not quite sure I heard you, or that you believe what you said. Say it once more please, little one, as though you believe it."

I stood on my naked toes to make myself as big as I could, raised both my hands toward heaven and shouted, "*I don't have to be afraid, because GOD is strong and will come to my rescue!*"

My shouting woke my grandmother, and she quickly made her displeasure known, but my grandfather nodded and smiled. He knelt down, looked into my eyes and said, "Mary, as soon as you and I were born someone hit us to make us cry, thinking they were being of help to us. Cruelty by others is a part of life from the moment we are born until the moment we die, but no one can make you a prisoner to fear unless you allow it. Just as no one can stop a bird from singing its song, no one can stop you from doing the same, except you. Now, go back to bed and sleep in peace, because you know GOD is strong and will always come to your rescue." When I woke the next morning, I felt almost like my old self—almost.

Around my twelfth birthday, I decided to study Torah so that I could better understand what GOD was requiring of me. I went to my grandfather, told him what I intended to do and asked him to teach me. When he told me no, I came up with a plan to change his mind.

I began sitting quietly beside him whenever he sat down to study, holding a small scroll in my hand, which I read to myself as he held and silently read from a larger scroll. On the third day, I asked him again to teach me Torah as he did to his students, and again he said no. When I asked why not I was told, "The Law is to be taught to sons, and to their sons."[176]

On the seventh day, I tried again.

"No."

The twelfth day I repeated my request.

"No" was his answer, and tearful pleading on my part made no difference.

Two weeks later, things changed when I repeated what the rabbi had said that morning in the synagogue. "The Torah is full of life-giving and life-shaping words that help us to more faithfully dedicate our lives to GOD, but how can I faithfully dedicate my life if I don't know all of what Torah says to do?"

My lessons began the next day.

---

[176] Deuteronomy 4:9b (21st Century King James Version contains the words "sons" and "sons' sons").

My grandparents had a terrible argument because of my grandfather's decision, my grandmother arguing that he should not do it, but he would not be moved.

Some years later, when others decided for me that the time had come for me to marry, GOD as my primary concern became a problem, for everyone except me. I found reasons to delay marriage because I was determined to wait for the husband I knew would best suit *me*. Someone who had GOD as his primary concern, who would treat me as his right hand rather than as his property, but the plans my grandparents had for me soon began to dominate the conversation, and overshadow the plans I had for myself.

### Life under Protective Custody

When several introductory meetings failed to produce any interest on my part, my grandparents chose a husband for me, leaving me with two choices. I could surrender to the life others were so carefully preparing for me, or I could choose a different way, and I chose the road less traveled.

Any student under the tutelage of a recognized and respected rabbi had the right to challenge an interpretation of the law by requesting a hearing before the local council, which had the authority to amend laws and issue judgments, as Moses had done. The road less traveled meant I would go before the Council and request a change in the marriage law, using debate tactics taught me by my grandfather, but from the moment of decision I knew the way would not be made easy.

My grandfather was a highly respected member of the Council, but when I put my plans before him, he told me forthrightly that I would receive neither help nor support from him, and that any consequences from my actions would be mine alone to bear, but he also promised never to deny being my rabbi.

It took a battle to get all the required documents signed and permissions granted. Sometimes I even thought of giving up because I was so weary, but my sense of mission that life was purposeful and important kept me pressing on, and standing upright. Many months passed before I was able to stand before the Council and present my case. I was very young and felt very frightened, but I was able to speak to the members with confidence because I was asking for the right reason, and because what I was asking for had such beneficial consequences for so many lives, including my own.

I said to the Council, "Honorable teachers, I stand before you today for the same reason you are here—we love and are guided by the Law of GOD, our faithful Counselor. I believe we all might also agree that there are times when the needs of a community outweigh the needs of any one individual living in that community, and that a wife is to honor her husband as a husband is to love his wife. Truly, I say to you, I have no greater desire than to be obedient to GOD and GOD's Law—but I struggle to understand how obedience to the Creator of all things means I must become the property of a man.

"How can it be that all of you get to decide for *me* what I should or should not do, have or become, just because I was born a woman? And why are my only choices to be those of living secluded and without benefit of power, voice or say in my grandparents' home, or being married off—perhaps even against my own will—to live secluded in the home of a husband without benefit of power, voice or say?"

No one tried to stop me from speaking, so I continued.

"No one present here today can deny the existence of two very different creation stories in Bereshit,[177] both of which explain the creation of man and woman. In the first story, the woman and man come forth at the same time, each having equal standing in GOD's sight, and each receiving the same commands. *This* is the arrangement that Torah says GOD described as being very good![178]

"In the second creation story, the man is created first and is given a more prominent position by the teller of the story, which appears

---

[177] "Genesis" in the English Bible.
[178] Genesis 1:27–32.

to be the interpretation this Council prefers! The difficulty arising from this different conviction is that the storyteller would have us believe GOD *first* created a man, and from the body of that man brought forth a woman! Honorable teachers, no disrespect is intended when I say that I have seen many women give birth to a man child—and many times over—but never have I seen a woman come from the body of a man![179]

A few of the rabbis laughed, until a look from the chief rabbi silenced them. Several of the others frowned and whispered to one another, but I acted as though I took no notice.

"I interpret the woman and the man being created together as signifying that each is fully independent and different—yet similar enough to be a proper fit for one another—created to function as one for the glory of GOD! What I hear in the reading of this first story is a scribe's description of how things are—or how they must, will or ought to be! What I hear in the second story is that a woman was a proper fit for a man who was not doing well alone.[180]

"Honorable teachers, I submit to you this day that GOD did not create a woman to stand silently, or subserviently, behind a man, but to stand beside him as his *ezer kenegdo*.[181] As the man's sustainer, helper

---

[179] Genesis 2:18–22.
[180] Genesis 2:18, 20b.
[181] Hebrew scholar Robert Alter says that the phrase "ezer kenegdo" is "is notoriously difficult to translate" (*The Hebrew Bible: A Translation with Commentary*, Vol.1, 14). Alter translates "ezer kenegdo" as "sustainer beside him." *Ezer* has also been interpreted as "helper" by other translators (i.e. ESV), but Alter says the word "help" is "too weak because it suggests a merely auxiliary [or inferior, subordinate or lesser] function . . ." He also points out that elsewhere in the Scriptures, "ezer" refers to an "active intervention on behalf of someone, especially in military contexts, as often [found] in Psalms" (i.e., 33:20, 91:4–5).

and keeper, as GOD is Israel's Sustainer, Helper and Keeper. Given the importance of a woman to the life and health of a man, and he to hers, should not, therefore, every woman have some say in who that man will be? To be able to choose him, as GOD chose Israel."

When I began asking the Council for a change in the marriage laws so that they might better reflect GOD's intent of equal footing and shared reliance between a woman and her husband, several of the rabbis began walking out of the room, but I continued to press my case.

"My request should not be unfamiliar to any of you. You no doubt may recall a similar situation concerning the daughters of Zelophehad, who died but left no living sons. His daughters—Maleh, Noah, Hoglah, Milcah, and Tirzah—went before Moses, Eleazar the priest and all the leaders and congregations to ask for a change in the inheritance law, so that they could inherit their father's estate and ensure their survival.[182] A change that would have benefited not only the daughters of Zelophehad, but all the daughters of Israel as well!

"Honorable teachers, the conclusion of the story you also know. Moses consulted with GOD about the matter and GOD ruled in the daughters' favor,[183] but a group of men who were unhappy with GOD's decision went to Moses to complain and Moses—without consulting GOD—added restrictive language to GOD's decree. It would be as GOD ordained—in the absence of sons women would have equal standing as inheritors—but Moses included wording that said all decisions about *who*

---

[182] Numbers 27:1-4.
[183] Numbers 27:8 (1–8).

the inheriting daughters could marry would remain subject to the decision of their closest male relative. [184]

"Honorable teachers, who benefits most from this arrangement? And what does Moses' decision to do what he did say about him—that he should side with men rather than with GOD?"

My grandfather was the last rabbi to leave, perhaps he was recalling that my own father had died leaving no living sons, meaning my closing words were to an empty room.

"What frightens all of you so about a woman engaging in celestial conversations? Why do you resist so strongly the image of a woman created as divine and free as a man. The two standing together and yet apart, helpers to one another, rather than owner and possession. Is there someone here who might be willing to answer my question?"

That night, in the middle of the night, I wrapped some food in my shawl and left home. I knew of only one other woman who had done what I was doing. From the day she left, her name was never spoken in public again, people simply referred to her as the one who went abroad, [185] the acceptable social expression for a prostitute, which became my lot as well.

---

[184] Numbers 36:3 (1–12).
[185] Jews for Jesus, "The Role of Women in the Bible," https://jewsforjesus.org/learn/the-role-of-women-in-the-bible (Accessed June 24, 2024), 2. "In Talmudic times, respectable women were expected to stay within the confines of the home. The terminology for a prostitute was 'one who goes abroad'."

My decision to leave the way I did—no money, very little food and no plan—was a reckless gamble, because I knew nothing about surviving on my own, but GOD took pity on me and rescued me.

Trial by Fire

I did my best to keep out of sight by traveling at night, often by the light of the moon, and staying hidden during the day. When my food was completely gone, I forced myself to go on. When hunger and thirst became more than I could bear, I stole food from other people's gardens and water from their wells, leaving a blessing and prayer of thanksgiving in return for what I had taken, but as the landscape turned from green to more desert-like conditions, opportunities to take what wasn't mine became few and far between.

My first real stretch of rib-clinging hunger lasted twelve days, and ended when my face brushed against some tree leaves as I was walking through the darkness. My first thought was that my weakened physical state had caused me to imagine a tree, but when I reached out my hand and my fingers touched leaves and branches, I knew the tree was real. One lone fig tree growing in a most unlikely place, like manna falling down from heaven.[186] I took a bite of its fruit and knew then what the goodness of GOD tasted like, and I ate until my stomach could hold nothing more. I wrapped as many figs as I could carry in my shawl, and for several days, I knew neither hunger nor thirst.

The decision to move at night and stay hidden during the day served me well. Until I decided to sit and watch a sunrise one morning,

---

[186] "Manna" is the miraculous bread from heaven that GOD provided for the Israelites during their journey to the land of Canaan. They complained of hunger and manna fell from the sky (Exodus 16:2-4, 11-15, 31, 35; Numbers 11:4-9, 21:5; Deuteronomy 8:1-3; Joshua 5:10-12; Psalm 78:21-24). Jesus explains how He is bread from heaven (John 3:16-17, 6:26-27, 32-33, 41, 47-51, Revelation 2:17).

and lingered too long out in the open. Three shepherd boys caught sight of me and came after me.

I tried to outrun them, but the terrain was rough and they quickly caught up to me. One of the boys grabbed my hair, pushed me to the ground, flipped me onto my back and stuffed a rag in my mouth to silence my screams. A second boy grabbed my arms and pinned them to the ground above my head, as the third boy yanked my legs apart with such force I thought they might separate from my body. The pain was unlike anything I had ever known, and my face was on fire from the heat of my tears. The boy shoved my dress up to my waist and exposed himself. As he was lowering himself onto my body and I began feeling his weight, I closed my eyes as tightly as I could to hide myself from what was happening, as I had covered my eyes that terrible day in the marketplace—and then my rescuer appeared.

*(Mary closes her eyes and is silent for several moments before continuing her testimony.)*

I felt the man's weight lifting off my body, and when I opened my eyes, I saw a large man dressed in fur standing behind him. He hit my would-be rapist on the side of his head with a large rock, rendering him unconscious, as the two other boys ran off into the desert. My deliverer helped me to my feet and stood with his arm around me, supporting me until I was steady again. When he asked if I was willing to go with him, I nodded yes. Not only because I could not yet speak from the trauma, but also because I had nowhere else to go.

Baptism by Water

Neither of us spoke as he led me to a nearby cave tucked into a hillside, the room was brightly lit by an open fire, around which sat several men. When they saw me, all conversation and movement ceased. At the sight of them, I began pulling back from going in, until my rescuer told me his name and explained their presence. "I am Rabbi Yochanan,[187] and these men are my disciples," language I understood, and my understanding calmed me.

One of the disciples began preparing a place for me alongside the wall where I could sleep. Another young man offered me a drink, and as he handed me the cup, it almost fell from his hand when my fingertips got too close to his. I fell asleep while someone else was preparing a plate of food for me. When I woke, it was dark outside. I did not know what to do with myself, as everyone else prepared to bed down for the night, the time I would normally be on the move. Thankfully, it only took a few days before my body returned to the habit of sleeping when most other people did.

Rabbi Yochanan was a Levite, whose priestly heritage came not only through his father, Zachariah, but also through his mother, Elizabeth.[188] Yet, there was nothing at all priestly-looking about him. His clothing was the bits and pieces of woolly remnant shed by camels, held together by a heavy leather rope tied around his waist and chest. He ate only fruit, wild honey and insects like grasshoppers, and he shunned

---

[187] The Hebrew name for "John."
[188] Luke 1:5–6 (5–13).

wine and strong drink. For the rabbi, GOD's Temple was the entire wilderness,[189] and that suited him. Much more so than the idea of him dressed in linen robes serving in the confines of a synagogue.

Yet, in other ways, rabbi Yochanan was more priest-like than any priest I had ever known, to that point. He said what he believed, believed what he said, and preached with such authority that people came from miles around to hear him tell about the kingdom of GOD and to be baptized, and his message was always the same. Repentance is the path leading to everlasting life, and the proper response to GOD's forgiveness of sins. The rabbi also had a warning for those who were using baptism like a spiritual safety net, instead of as the gateway to a new life. "Every tree that does not bear good fruit will be cut down and thrown into the fire, and even now the blade of the ax is aimed at the root of the tree!"[190] The rabbi understood his work, purpose and mission.

Some months after my rescue, I took my turn at the front of the baptismal line. When the rabbi gestured for me to come forward, I carefully walked down a sloping bank into the water, stepping lightly across the river's rocky bottom, until I stood between him and his assistant. Rabbi Yochanan looked into my eyes and repeated to me the same words he spoke to every person passing that way. "I baptize you with water, but there is Someone coming who will baptize you with the Holy Spirit."[191] As the two men gently tilted my body backward, I closed my eyes and held my breath as they submerged me beneath the surface of

---

[189] Matthew 3:4, 11:18a; Mark 1:6; Luke 1:13, 7:33 (see also Deuteronomy 18:1–8 and 2 Kings 1:7–8).
[190] Matthew 3:1–3, 7–10; Mark 1:4–5, 7; Luke 3:2–14. "Fruit" in this case are the works, deeds, or behaviors of human conduct, like fruit that grows from the planting of seeds.
[191] Matthew 3:11; Luke 3:16.

the cool water. For the briefest of moments, it felt as though I was in another world and, just as quickly, they lifted me out of the river, water streaming down my body, soaked to the core, feeling like what a newly born baby must feel. Except no one hit me this time.

Over many months, while I was in rabbi Yochanan's company, never once did he ask me anything about myself, nor did I freely release any information. After my baptism, the time felt right to tell him my story.

I found him one day sitting alone on a rock, staring off into the distance. I waited to the side until he gestured for me to take a seat, and then I told the rabbi how I ended up in the place where he found me. I told him about my parents, my grandparents, about that terrible day in the marketplace, about wanting to learn Torah, about petitioning the council, and the fig tree. When I finally stopped talking, I waited for him to say something, but he said nothing. So much time passed, I began to wonder if he had even been listening—or worse—that he had been listening and was wondering what now to do with me.

When the rabbi picked up a small stick and began drawing in the dirt, I began mentally preparing myself for rejection, but the words he spoke put all my concerns to rest.

"The heart of the wise is in the house of mourning, surely oppression drives the wise into madness, but better is the end of a thing than its beginning. The patient in spirit is better than the proud in spirit, do not be quick in your spirit to become angry, for anger lodges in the bosom of fools. In time, you will not even remember those days of your life, because GOD is going to keep you occupied with a joy that will one day fill your heart." [192]

I did not know it at the time, but I was listening to prophecy. Praise GOD, I lived to see it come to be.

---

[192] Ecclesiastes 5:20, 7:4, 7–9 (ESV); Psalm 51:17.

## The Handover

For a long while, I never spoke when the rabbi's disciples were discussing and debating the Law, not until I heard someone say something I thought was contrary to the law, and gave in to the urge to speak my mind so that all could hear. When I did, the room became quiet and still, and the rabbi smiled and nodded, but the quietness lasted only a moment before the disciples began deliberating my words, and I felt as though I truly belonged. Living under the rabbi's authority made it possible for me to live the life I had once imagined for myself. I had no husband, of course, but I was with men who treated me no more and no less than they treated one another, as a trusted companion. I had a voice and a say, and I was free to become the best parts of myself. Even my disappearance a few days each month became part of the comfortable rhythm of our life together.

If the decision had been mine, I would have stayed with rabbi Yochanan always. I had no desire that anything should change, which may be part of the reason he handed me over. He understood, even though I did not at the time, that my life had not gone as far as GOD intended it should go. There were still other levels of glory for me to climb.

Over time, the rabbi's preaching reputation spread as far north as Jerusalem, and wherever he traveled, whenever people heard he was coming, they found their way to him. When the people came after hearing news that he had set up camp near Bethany,[193] they spoke of

---

[193] John 1:28; Matthew 3:5.

leaving tools lying in the fields and household chores left undone in the middle of a workday, to come and be baptized.

A rumor began spreading that rabbi Yochanan was Israel's long-awaited Messiah, his disciples and I had whispered about this possibility among ourselves, but no one dared to ask him directly. Neither were we surprised when Jewish authorities in Jerusalem sent a delegation of priests to examine the rabbi's credentials and ask the question on everyone's mind. "Just who are you?"[194]

He responded by telling them who he was not. "I am not the Savior, nor am I Elijah or the prophet spoken of by Moses. I am the one of whom Isaiah spoke—the one shouting in the wilderness trying to help make a people ready for the coming of the Lord!" and all of the rabbi's words were reported by the delegation to the ones who had sent them.[195]

The visit from the authorities triggered something in the rabbi. The next day he began sitting near the entrance of Bethany's marketplace at a certain time each day, searching the faces of men who were coming and going, as though he was looking for one face in particular. The disciples and I took turns sitting with him in pairs of two, in case he needed anything. The looks people gave me whenever they saw me sitting there, I learned to ignore, like light shining on an untroubled mind.

On one such day, as Andrew and I sat on either side of the rabbi, a craving for figs drove me into the marketplace, and I went alone. The merchant put the two pieces of fruit on the counter. I suppose not wanting to accidentally touch me. When I picked up the figs they were

---

[194] John 1:19-22.
[195] Isaiah 40:3; John 1:19–27; Matthew 3:3; Mark 1:2–3; Luke 1:16–17, 3:2–6.

warm from the sun, and when I held them beneath my nose and inhaled the sweet, sweet fragrance, the aroma was so intoxicating I closed my eyes in pure delight, and my lips curved into a smile. Blinded by this bliss, I turned to leave and almost collided with a man. When I looked up and opened my mouth to apologize, I found myself looking into a pair of dark, soulful eyes that were staring back at me. The feeling that washed over me at that moment I had no name for, or understanding of, because I had never experienced that kind of feeling before.

I could not stop myself from returning both the man's smile and his gaze, but the disapproving sounds and faces around us reminded us where we were. I ducked around him and walked away, nibbling on a fig and trying not to look back, but when I did look, I was pleased to see he was still looking at me. For the rest of the day, I tried not to think anything more about him, or about how he made me feel, but I thought about that man well into the night.

Seven days later, Andrew and I were again sitting with the rabbi when he pointed to a man and said, "There He is—the One I have been telling all of you about—the One I said was to come after me, but is before me. I know this because the One who sent me to baptize with water told me the Messiah would come to me for baptism, at which time I would know His identity so that I could reveal it to all of Israel. That Man came to me for baptism, and with my own eyes, I saw the Spirit of GOD come down to rest On Him and it remained on Him. The two of you are my witnesses that I have confirmed His identity and of all that I have said to you."[196]

I looked closely at the Man to whom the rabbi was pointing and recognized Him as the same Man with whom I had almost collided at the fig stand.

The next day, Andrew and I were handed-over into the care of Rabbi Yeshua of Nazareth.[197] The day after that, we began the journey from Bethany to Andrew's hometown in Bethsaida.

I tried my best to be angry with rabbi Yochanan for handing me over to another man without asking for either my opinion or consent, as though I was nothing more than property, but I could not stay angry for very long. There was too much happiness inside me because the rabbi had handed me over to this particular Man.

---

[196] John 1:29–36; Matthew 3:13–17; Mark 1:9–11; Luke 3:21–22. Mary Magdalene is presented here as one of two unnamed disciples in John 1:35, 37 (Andrew is named in verse 40). The "dove" mentioned at Jesus's baptism reminds me of the dove associated with Noah and the remnant of GOD's creatures being saved for a new creation (Genesis 8:6–12).
[197] John 1:37, 40.

### The Hem of His Garment

The one hundred mile journey to Bethsaida took seven days to complete, and was not without its problems, but two matters took me completely by surprise. Andrew revealed a side of himself I had not seen before, and the Rabbi Yeshua and I became quite taken with one another.

Among all of rabbi Yochanan's disciples, Andrew was the one everyone admired and looked up to. He was responsible, self-assured, had a good mind with a dry sense of humor, and was not easily persuaded, but as we traveled toward his hometown, he became a shadow of his former self and refused to talk about much of anything other than his brother Simon.

According to Andrew, Simon was not only a gifted, driven and outspoken man of action who would be of great help to Rabbi Yeshua's ministry, there was apparently nothing Simon could not do or do better than most. By Andrew's account, Simon was everything Andrew was not, and the closer we got to Bethsaida, the more praise Simon received. It was, in some ways, disturbing to see this other side of Andrew, and yet it was good to see as well, because it allowed me a glimpse inside the backstory that gave rise to his lifelong deference to Simon.

Love is the other matter that took me by surprise.

In the evening hours, after Andrew retired, Yeshua and I would sit talking in low voices late into the night. I liked that He understood Himself and I loved His laugh, which was deep, soft and warm all at the same time. We were attracted to each other in ways I think neither of us expected, it gave us pleasure just to sit and look into each other's eyes. We were so completely at ease in each other's presence, that by the time we reached Bethsaida, we shared an unspoken understanding between us.

As soon as we reached the city, Andrew went in search of his brother, as Yeshua and I searched for fresh water. When a kind woman offered us some from her well, we drew what we needed and found a shade tree to sit under.

He poured some of the water into a bowl and placed it between us. As we were leaning forward to scoop some of it into our hands, our heads collided, making us both laugh. I was reaching out to try again when He took hold of my hands, placed them in the water, and began rubbing and caressing my fingers to clean them. It was our first time touching one another. My heart was pounding so hard I dared not look at Him, lest He see in my eyes what I was feeling. When my hands were clean, He patted them dry with the hem of the outer garment He was wearing.

He took off my sandals and placed my feet in the water, working His fingers in between my toes to remove the dust and dirt that had gathered there. My eyes closed and a smile came to my lips, as He rubbed the soreness and tiredness in my feet away and then gently dried them.

I emptied the bowl and poured in some fresh water, took Yeshua's hands in mine and guided them into the water, ministering to Him as He had to me, and then did the same to His feet. I emptied the bowl again and filled it with fresh water, which we used to clean one another's faces, and these acts of serving one another in this way connected us even more deeply. Exactly what happened between us that day I cannot put into words, except to say that we became inseparable from that point on.

When Andrew finally returned with Simon, it was an interesting moment. Rather than being introduced, as was the custom, Simon bowed and introduced himself, and the look Yeshua gave him was priceless.

"So *you* are Simon, Yochanan's son,[198] He said. "As of today, your new name will be Cephas,"[199] and I was caught off guard. Neither Andrew nor rabbi Yochanan had ever said a word about their family ties.

The next day Andrew, Cephas and I accompanied Yeshua to Galilee in search of a man named Philip, who was also from Bethsaida but not known to either Andrew or Cephas. Rabbi Yochanan had passed on the name while we were still in Bethany, along with a strong recommendation. Philip, in turn, introduced Yeshua to Nathanael,[200] bringing the number of His disciples to five, including me.

---

[198] I have used artistic license to associate the "John" mentioned in John 1:42b with rabbi Yochanan.
[199] Cephas is "Peter" in the English Bible.
[200] John 1:43–45.

### Mary, the Mother of Yeshua

Three days after finding Philip and Nathanael, we arrived in Cana to attend a wedding,[201] which is where I met Yeshua's mother for the first time. Her name, too, was Mary.

Their joy at seeing one another again was unmistakable. Mary flung her arms around her Son's neck as He wrapped His arms around her and lifted her off the ground and twirled her around and around. "Put me down! Put me down!" she protested, but everyone watching knew she was delighted beyond measure to hold her Son again, and He her.

Any worries I had about how she might receive me—and I had them—had been wasted time. Mary looked at her Son, then at me and back at Him again, as though searching for something inside each of us, and in us together. When she reached up and patted our cheeks with her rough and calloused hands, I saw nothing but contentment on her face. When she grabbed me by my waist and pulled me away to help with the wedding preparations, I knew she was embracing me as family.

Cana is where I also first witnessed GOD's power in motion through Mary's Son.

At some point during the wedding celebration, Yeshua's mother came to tell Him all the wine jugs were empty, as though she expected Him to do something about it, but He rebuffed her with two words. "Woman, please," and I thought the matter over and done with, until I

---

[201] John 2:1.

saw Yeshua do exactly as His mother had hinted He should do. He turned several jugs of plain water into fine wine, but among the people who heard their exchange, only I seemed surprised by the outcome. His mother certainly was not. After telling Him about the wine, she instructed the servants to do whatever He told them to do, and then went back to serving guests.[202]

After the wedding, we headed next for Capernaum, accompanied by Yeshua's mother and two of His brothers.[203] I was glad to have her traveling with us, because we were able to use that time together to become better acquainted. Over many evenings, we asked and answered question after question, as we sat together in front of a warm fire. On our final evening together, wanting to know more about Yeshua's childhood, I asked Mary about His father, and several minutes passed before she answered me.

"When Joseph and I were still in our season of engagement, before we were officially married, I was visited in a dream by an angel who told me I would give birth to a holy Child conceived by the power and Spirit of GOD, and that the Child was to be named Yeshua. I did not know, or really understand, how what the angel said was to happen, was going to come to be. I was a young girl. I had never known a man in any intimate way, nor how children came to be. I was also frightened, too, by the thought of what other people would think and say about me, especially Joseph, but I freely said yes to GOD's will for my life.[204]

---

[202] John 2:2–11.
[203] John 2:12.
[204] Luke 1:26–35.

"When I knew for certain that I was with Child, I told Joseph, but he couldn't bring himself to believe what I told him had happened. All he knew was that the Child growing inside me could not possibly be his. His plan was to withdraw from our engagement quietly in order to spare me as much humiliation as possible, but he changed his mind after also being visited in a dream by an angel, who told Joseph he had been chosen as the man GOD trusted to take on the responsibility of protecting me and the Child I was carrying. Joseph told me that's what he intended to do, and protecting us is exactly what he did."[205]

I asked Mary if Yeshua had ever spoken to her about Joseph's leaving, and again she gave thought to my question before answering.

"No, He didn't. One morning my husband left our home as usual and just never came back, and Yeshua was the only one of my children who showed neither surprise nor concern. By GOD's grace, everyone was old enough to help care for our home, themselves and each other, but your question reminds me of something more. The timing of Joseph leaving followed a disagreement between him and Yeshua. Joseph wanted Him to spend more time involved in the family's carpentry business, to help bring money into the household, but my Son preferred spending His time with religious teachers, or alone with GOD. When Joseph reminded Yeshua that he was His father and about His promise to obey,[206] Yeshua said to him, "GOD is my Father, and my Father thanks you for your service Joseph." The next morning, my husband said goodbye and never returned.

---

[205] Matthew 1:18–25, 2:13–15, 19–23.
[206] Luke 2:51a (41–52).

"I've chosen to understand Joseph's departure in this way. He was a good and righteous man who gave up the life he had planned for himself, in order to serve GOD. I was proud to be his wife, and I take great comfort in believing that his leaving was also part of the LORD'S plan—that GOD included time just for Joseph—because he never would have left us had GOD not given him leave to go. He was skilled enough to make a living anywhere he went, and so I trusted and believed in my heart that he went with GOD's blessing."

When I asked Mary how she knew Yeshua was going to do what she wanted Him to do, to make more wine for the wedding guests, she laughed. "If He calls you 'woman',[207] it's either because He's trying to cover His own emotions, or to chastise you in love. He was chastising me that day, because I was asking in a very public way for Him to do what He normally resisted doing publicly. But the word never, ever means He doesn't care or won't respond."

In many ways, Yeshua mirrored Joseph's faithfulness, discipline and skillfulness as a carpenter, but His mother marked Him. Watching her endure the indignities of poverty while raising her children is how He intimately understood the plight of the poor. Seeing her flourish despite her circumstances prepared Him to teach others how to transcend poverty's limitations.

During our last night in Capernaum, we overheard a group of local men discussing the worsening civil conflict going on between Jewish rebels and Rome's soldiers. Conditions for the poor had become unbearable, almost squalid-like, they said. Not only were they being

---

[207] John 4:21, 20:15; Matthew 15:28; Luke 13:12.

asked to bear a double portion of burdens—including taxes—they were being neglected by the priests and religious elite, who were busy bending a knee to the Roman emperor. I saw a deep crease form on Yeshua's forehead, but He said nothing. Only after His mother retired for the night did He announce we would leave the next day for Jerusalem.[208]

We set out early the next morning, traveling in a boat given to Yeshua as a gift by the host of the wedding in Cana, but He left His brothers and mother behind, with plans to meet up with them again in a month or so. What He did not say was that our first port of call would be Magdala.

---

[208] John 2:13.

## The Test

When I realized the direction the boat was going, I looked at Yeshua, but He would not look at me. My feelings were hurt, and I felt angry and betrayed, because I could think of no reason why He would take me back to Magdala, but I said nothing. When the boat came to rest alongside the pier, I busied myself tying lines and helping bring down the sails, before settling in the bow with my back to the others.

I tried to convince myself that we had stopped for supplies, except no one left the boat, and we had all the supplies we needed. Every reason I could think of for why we were in Magdala were put to rest by one logical objection after another—except one. I finally realized we were there because chance would play no part in Yeshua's life. The hours we spent tied to the dock were to give me enough time to make a different choice, if I wanted to. He knew what lay ahead, even if I did not. Maybe not that year or even the next, but one day, and He was offering me a way to bow out, free of judgment and questions. Magdala could be my point of departure before things got bad.

When I realized this, I made my way from my corner of solitude to go and sit by Yeshua's side. A short time later He called out, "Prepare to cross to the other side!"[209] I threw off my shawl and joined Andrew and Cephas in hoisting up the sails, and they eyed me again as though not quite believing what they were seeing.

As we were pulling out of Capernaum earlier that morning, the brothers had been quite astonished to see that I could handle a boat. Cephas made it out to be a much bigger thing than it was, until I

---

[209] Mark 5:1.

reminded him and his brother that I, too, had grown up on the sea. "Or did you suppose my only skill lay in cooking the fish?" I asked, and even Cephas laughed.

Yeshua was not a fisher, but He had a knack for knowing exactly where to find schools of fish. His other skill was that what He could not fix, He could make brand new. Many times, I watched Him take a lump of wood and create something beautiful and useful, and everything He created reflected the beauty that was inside of Him. Nathanael and Philip were also inexperienced with boats, but they learned the ropes by handling them.

As we prepared to cross to the other side, the two friends untied the lines securing us to the pier in Magdala, tossed them into the hull and made the short leap back into the boat, as Cephas navigated the vessel away from my hometown. When we cleared the dock, he steered the boat toward a Gentile region known as the Decapolis, as Yeshua wrapped His robe around His body and settled down to sleep.

In the area where we were crossing, it was normal for storms to appear suddenly, so that when clear blue skies turned gray and the waves became choppy, neither Andrew, Cephas nor I became unduly alarmed. We all agreed that the changing weather posed no immediate threat to us.

Near the midway crossing point, the gray sky darkened and the waves became rougher, causing the boat to bob and weave more dangerously. A gust of wind came from nowhere and nearly capsized the boat, which was rocking so violently and dipping so low into the sea that water was pouring into it. Andrew and I rushed to bring down the sails before they torn apart, as Cephas tried to hold the waterlogged boat steady and Philip and Nathanael did their best to bail out water.

In between claps of thunder and flashes of lightning, Andrew and Cephas kept shouting, "Teacher, we're drowning! Help us! Help us! Don't you care?" because the threat of drowning was very real.

When Yeshua awakened, He uncurled His body in an unhurried way and stood to His feet, swaying from side to side with the movement of the waves, balancing Himself as though riding the storm itself. He turned to face the blowing wind and rain and shouted, "Be still!" and immediately the wind began to subside. The downpour transformed into a misty rain, and the water calmed itself. The waves began to lap gently against the sides of the boat, and the sky turned a light shade of blue. As though nature itself was saying, "I'm sorry."

Yeshua turned to look at the five of us and asked, "Where is your faith in me?"[210]

The look of disappointment I saw on His face that day has always stayed with me, and that was the moment I decided that I would never again be the reason for that look. When I went to Yeshua to apologize and ask His forgiveness, Philip saw us kiss,[211] and when he went and huddled with the others, I assumed he was telling them all about it. Then again, it may well be they were whispering about a Rabbi who even the wind and waves obeyed.[212]

That was the second time I witnessed the power of GOD in motion through Mary's Son.

---

[210] Matthew 8:23–26; Mark 4:35–41; Luke 8:22–25a.
[211] Marvin Meyer, trans., "The Gospel of Philip," *The Nag Hammadi Scriptures: The Revised and Updated Translation of Sacred Gnostic Tests, Complete in One Volume*, ed. Marvin Meyer (New York: HarperCollins, 2007), 171.
[212] Matthew 8:27; Mark 4:41; Luke 8:25a.

When everything was happening, I did not understand that the seemingly impossible things Yeshua was able to do were signs testifying to His faith and trust in GOD. I knew only that I wanted my own faith and trust to become as deep.

I never really believed that Yeshua was actually sleeping as soundly as we all thought He was. No human being could have slept through that kind of storm, and for all His faith and power, Yeshua was still flesh and blood. I came to believe that He was waiting, as He waited two days before leaving after receiving the news that His dear friend Lazarus was dead.[213]

---

[213] John 11:6 (1–44).

## The Garden

When we reached the other side of the Sea of Galilee we anchored the boat near Gerasene, and Yeshua went ashore to minister to an ill man.[214] He returned a few days later, and we continued on to Jerusalem.

After arriving, as the men were setting up camp, Yeshua took me to an olive grove located about a half mile outside the walls of Jerusalem. Years earlier, He had stumbled across it during one of His family's Passover pilgrimages,[215] and at the center of the grove was a most beautiful garden, His personal sanctuary.

Three days later, He went to the temple alone. When He returned to camp, an entire crowd was with Him, all of whom were talking about something that happened in the marketplace involving Yeshua and a whip. A young man named Judas Iscariot was among them, and from him we were able to learn the details of what happened. When the excitement finally quieted down, Yeshua had disappeared, and when He did not return by evening time, I felt almost certain I knew where He might be.

I found Him in His garden, lying prostrate in prayer, bathed in moonlight, His forehead pressed to the ground, arms stretched out to the side.

When He finally sat upright and saw me sitting there, He did not look surprised. I asked Him if He was well, but He did not answer, so I sat beside Him and put my arm around His shoulders. When He moved

---

[214] Mark 5:1–20.
[215] Luke 2:41.

to sit between my thighs and rest His head between my breasts, I folded my arms around His neck, draped my hands across His chest and rested my head against His. Neither of us spoke for some time, but it was a comfortable silence. The kind that does not need words to give it meaning.

When He finally spoke, He asked me a question for which I had no answer. "Mary," He said, "if you knew you didn't have long to live, how would you spend your remaining time?"

Three years after we first entered His garden together Yeshua was arrested there.

## The Execution

Yeshua was once a well-respected Rabbi and much admired Man, who became one of the most rejected men on Earth. The crowds of people who once hung on to His every word began turning away and against Him, not because of any unfaithfulness on His part, but because they grew disturbed and offended by things they could not see and did not understand. A few left to chase after other men who promised more and better things in the here and now. Things got so bad near the end, Yeshua thought it necessary to ask each of His disciples whether they, too, planned to stay or go.[216] He needed to know for certain, because chance could play no part in the making of His plans, and I assumed He never asked me because I had already answered the question.

When Philip arrived with news about what had happened, Yeshua's mother, His sister Mary, and I were together.[217]

Philip told us that after leaving the last supper we all shared, the Teacher had taken them to their regular meeting place in the garden, all except Judas. They were waiting for the Teacher to speak, but He kept pacing back and forth, which is how they knew something was wrong. The more time that passed the more restless and distressed He became, saying He wanted to die because He felt so alone.

---

[216] John 6:53–61, 66–67; 7:23.

[217] According to Marvin Meyer, *The Gospel of Philip*, p. 167, "Three women always walked with the master: Mary his mother, <his> sister, and Mary of Magdala, who is called his companion. For 'Mary' is the name of his sister, his mother, and his companion." John 19:25 identifies the third Mary as the sister of Yeshua's mother."

When I heard that, a sound came out of me that I cannot describe. I wrapped my arms around my body to hold in the pain of knowing He felt alone and abandoned, and to comfort myself, because I was helpless to do anything about anything. When Philip said some of the other brothers had confessed to falling asleep instead of praying for their Teacher, as He asked them to do,[218] my tears began falling and Yeshua's mother and sister began weeping as well.

Philip blamed Judas Iscariot for Yeshua's arrest, saying, "He betrayed the Teacher by bringing His enemies straight to Him, and then had the arrogance to greet the Rabbi with a kiss! What kind of friend betrays another friend with a kiss, and why, in the name of heaven itself, would the Teacher call Judas His friend?"[219] I knew then that events had unfolded according to the plan Yeshua had put in place. What I did not know until that moment was which disciple would hand Him over to the authorities.

I said to Philip, "And now? Where is the Teacher now?"

He said, "As I speak, Roman soldiers are taking Him to be executed."

With her mother sheltered between us, Mary and I pushed our way through a procession of people, trying to get close enough to lay our eyes on Yeshua, and when we finally saw Him, He was drenched in

---

[218] John 18:1; Matthew 26:30–46; Mark 14:26–41; Luke 22:39–46 (the mention of Jesus's "sweat like great drops of blood" in Luke 22:44 is a rare medical condition called hematidrosis).
[219] John 18:4 (2–4); Luke 22:47–48; Matthew 26:47–50a; Mark 14:43–45.

blood from head to toe, His scourging[220] so violent, His back was nothing more than ribbons of flesh. He was stumbling, barely able to stand, as He tried to carry a solid beam of wood across His shoulders. I had to force myself not to think about the pain He had to feel from the coarse wood rubbing against His open wounds.

When Yeshua fell and could not get up again on His own strength, one of the soldiers pulled a man from the crowd and made him carry the cross beam the remainder of the way,[221] as two other soldiers half-carried and half-dragged Yeshua behind him.

At the site of execution, they threw Him face down into the dirt, connected the crossbeam to a long vertical wood beam, and began to crucify Him.

Two soldiers each used a foot to push Yeshua onto His back, then dragged Him by the arms onto the crossbeam so that His shoulders lay flat across it and His arms were stretched out to either side. Each laid a knee across His arms and pressed down with their weight to hold Yeshua still, as two other soldiers put weight on His legs. A fifth soldier pounded a six-inch nail into each of His wrists and tied His arms to the wooden beam with leather ropes. The soldiers holding down His legs bent them at the knees so His feet were flat against the long beam, one

---

[220] Matthew 27:26. Scourging is a beating with a lead-tipped whip called a flagrum or flagellum. The whip had three separate cords, each of which had three or more round balls of lead and/or bits of bone attached, which would rip through a victim's flesh. Among Jews, this type of whipping was limited to forty lashes, but Rome had no such limitation.
[221] Matthew 27:32; Luke 23:26. The crossbeam or "patibulum."

foot on top of the other, as a six-inch nail was beat into His heel and foot, anchoring Him to the long beam, and He was in great agony. Working together, the soldiers lifted Yeshua into the air and the long beam slid into a waiting open hole in the ground. The force of the drop made Him yell out in pain.[222]

As His breathing became more and more distressed, Yeshua kept pressing His feet against the long beam to push His body upward, high enough to open His airway and snatch a breath of air, before the weight of His body would force His knees to bend and chin to fall, closing off His airway again. We watched Him struggle this way for many hours. To add insult to injury, some of the religious rulers responsible for the crucifixion, who had been standing silently at a distance, began walking among the people and ridiculing Yeshua's suffering, saying, "He was so good at rescuing other people, let Him rescue Himself if He's GOD's Savior!"[223] Off in the distance were some of the other women who also loved Him,[224] which gave His mother, sister and I some measure of comfort.

Near the end, just before He was unable to push Himself up anymore to breathe, Yeshua made two things clear. He let me know that He loved me, and He made me responsible for the care of His mother.[225] When I knew He could see me, it was just for a moment in the midst of His pain, I nodded my head, praying that He understood I loved Him,

---

[222] John 19:18; Matthew 27:35; Mark 15:24; Luke 23:33.
[223] Matthew 27:42–44 (See also Psalm 22:8).
[224] Matthew 27:55; Luke 23:49; Mark 15:40.
[225] John 19:26-27.

too, and that I would watch over and care for His mother so long as she should live.

I thought I heard Him whisper, "I thirst," so I begged a soldier standing nearby to give Him something to drink. The man threw a filthy sponge into a bucket containing a foul-smelling substance, stabbed it with the tip of his spear and raised his weapon to Yeshua's lips.[226]

Praise GOD, He was already dead.

(*Mary drops her head and works to control her emotions*)

I learned later that the Sanhedrin Council had attempted to force Pilate, the governor of Rome, to change the language on a banner he had ordered be nailed at the top of Yeshua's cross, but Pilate ruled the banner would stand as written. "Yeshua of Nazareth, King of the Jews."[227]

I had hoped never to revisit those days. I testify about them today so that all may know the true cost of GOD's gifts of freedom and salvation.

---

[226] John 19:26–27; Matthew 27:48; Mark 15:36; Luke 23:36 (also Psalm 69:21).
[227] John 19:19–22; Matthew 27:37; Mark 15:31–32; Luke 23:38.

## The Burial

Caiaphas and the Jewish council had demanded Pilate to remove all dead bodies from the crosses before Shabbat arrived. When the afternoon sun signaled the lateness of the hour, it wasn't long before the soldiers began moving from one cross to the next, breaking the legs of anyone still left alive to hurry their death along. When they approached Yeshua to do the same to Him, I told them He was already dead. To make certain, one of the soldiers thrust the tip of his spear into the side of His body to make certain, and blood and water came rushing out of the wound.[228] When there was no reaction, they moved on to the next body, but our difficulty remained. His body had to come down and soon, otherwise the soldiers would do it for us, meaning they would toss Him aside like trash and leave His body for the buzzards to pick apart His flesh, but to remove Him from the cross we needed help. Never could I have imagined it would come by way of two members of the very Council that had demanded His execution.

Joseph of Arimathea was the first to appear, and he carried with him a set of white linen burial cloths and an official document granting him permission to claim Yeshua's body for burial. Joseph was a secret Believer who he hid his beliefs from the other council members, for fear of what they might do should they find out. He argued, he said, against them doing what they had done. When they ignored and rejected his warnings, Joseph said he refused to go along with their plans.[229]

He and I were discussing what to do next, and Mary was comforting her mother, when Nicodemus arrived carrying burial spices.

---

[228] John 19:31–34.
[229] John 19:38; Matthew 27:57–58; Mark 15:42–46; Luke 23:50–52.

He, too, had been a secret follower, visiting Yeshua in private late at night, he said, to keep the relationship concealed from the other council members. During one of those late night conversations is when Nicodemus said he became convinced the Council was wrong regarding the Rabbi from Nazareth and he, too, refused to go along with the Council's decision. He had watched the crucifixion from a distance, and had come now to help bury Yeshua, because he was determined to bear witness about the truth of what had been done.[230]

Yeshua's body was hanging no more than about six feet off the ground, but that was still too high to reach Him as we needed to, so we came up with a plan. As the smaller of the two men, Nicodemus climbed onto Joseph's shoulders, wrapped his legs around Joseph's neck and was hoisted him into the air. Nicodemus then threaded the large burial cloth beneath Yeshua's arms, draping it such that it could serve as a sling to lower His body to the ground. I handed Nicodemus a metal tool left behind by the soldiers and he extracted the nails from Yeshua's wrists, when he handed it back to me, I removed the nail binding His feet. We could not think about what we were doing, we had to focus the whole of our minds on doing what we had to do.

As Nicodemus lowered Yeshua's body, I raised my arms to help guide Him to the ground, where His mother was waiting to hold Him one last time, for as long as she could. After Nicodemus climbed down from Joseph's shoulders, we all stood by quietly as Mary cradled her Son in her arms, and we waited as long as we dared. Until Nicodemus gently reminded us about the lateness of the hour.

---

[230] John 3:2 (1–21), 7:50–52, 19:39.

He and Joseph took Yeshua from His mother's arms and laid Him on the large burial cloth. His sister tied the smaller linen cloth around His head and neck, as I walked around His body sprinkling the sweet-smelling spices. When Yeshua's mother began speaking, we paused our work to listen.

"Even though it's mixed with the other spices, I can smell the fragrance of the myrrh. My husband Joseph and I were in Judea for the yearly registration when I went into labor. He took me to an inn, so that I might have comfortable surroundings for the birth, but the innkeeper told us there was no room available, or was it that there was no room for poor people like us. That was the first, and only, time I ever saw Joseph cry, but GOD provided. A kind man who overheard what the innkeeper said took us home with him and Yeshua was born in his stable. Joseph cut His cord, washed Him with salt and oil, wrapped Him tightly with pieces of cloth and laid Him in a trough, where the animals usually fed. Three strangers brought us gifts of gold, frankincense and myrrh, which Joseph and I did not know what to make of it, but the gifts proved to be providential blessings.[231]

"From the moment He was born, Yeshua's life was in danger. For a time, Joseph and I even went into hiding in Egypt in order to protect my Son.[232] As refugees, and by law, we were required to register with the government, but we could not risk anyone finding out where we were. Being unregistered meant Joseph could not legally work—and this is how I know nothing just occurs to GOD—the gifts we received from the strangers is how we were able to survive. The gold we used to pay for

---

[231] Luke 2:1-7; Matthew 2:1-2, 11b (1–12).
[232] Matthew 2:13–15.

food and other necessary things, the frankincense was our incense for worship, and the myrrh was our medicine."

Mary looked as though she might have said more, but Joseph interrupted with a word of apology to tell us about an empty tomb he owned in a garden nearby where we could bury Yeshua. His mother walked behind us as Nicodemus, Joseph, Mary and I carried His linen-wrapped body to the burial site. We placed it inside the tomb, then secured and sealed the entrance to the cave as best as we could with large stones.[233] It was a rushed affair because the law forbid funerals on the Sabbath, the beginning of which was rapidly approaching, and we could not delay it for fear of leaving His body exposed where someone with ill intent might find it.

Joseph and Nicodemus were the first to leave, and Yeshua's mother and sister departed soon after, but I felt no urgency to leave, because Yeshua was Lord even of the Sabbath.[234]

I sat on the ground a short distance away from the tomb until evening transformed into dark night, and then I made my way home to wait for the third day[235] to come.

---

[233] Matthew 27:59–61; Mark 15:46–47: Luke 23:53–54.
[234] Matthew 12:8; Mark 2:27–28; Luke 6:5.
[235] Matthew 16:21, 17:9, 23, 20:18–19, 27:63; Mark 8:31, 9:9, 31, 10:34b; Luke 9:22, 18:33, 24:21.

The Third Day

Early in the morning on the third day, I went back to the tomb, and nothing was as we had left it.[236]

The stones we used to seal the entrance were sitting off to the side, and Yeshua's body was gone. The tomb was completely empty, except for the two pieces of linen cloths used to wrap His head and body. The larger cloth was lying exactly where His body had rested, the smaller piece was neatly folded and lying in a different section of the tomb.[237]

I ran back to town as fast as I could, to where I thought the brothers would most likely be, and found the door locked.[238] I pounded on it as I called out, "It's me, Mary! Let me in!" I heard the bolt moving, and when the door opened, Cephas was standing there. I told him what had happened, he told the others to put the lock back in place, then he and I ran together back to the tomb.

When we arrived at the cave, Cephas paused for the briefest of moments before ducking his head and stepping inside. When he came out a short time later, he had a look of confusion on his face, and described to me exactly what I had seen. We stood beside each other for a little while without speaking, and then he left and headed back to town.

Shortly after that is when Yeshua appeared to me in His risen state of glory.

---

[236] John 20:1 (also see Matthew 28:2; Mark 16:4; Luke 24:2 for other versions).
[237] John 20:5-7.
[238] John 20:2-4. See 20:19 for a reference to the locked door.

I ran again back to the house to tell the other disciples the good news about His resurrection, and to deliver the message He'd given me to tell them, but none of the brothers would believe anything I told them.[239]

Nor did they believe any of the other women who also reported seeing Yeshua alive,[240] because Cephas had already given them a different testimony.

---

[239] Mark 16: 9–11 (Some of the earliest scripture manuscripts—and some contemporary Bible translations—do not include 16:9-20).
[240] Luke 24:10–11.

The Sightings

Some say I did not immediately recognize Yeshua when He first appeared to me after His resurrection because my tears blinded me, but this is not so. At least not entirely. There were tears in my eyes, yes, but Yeshua's physical appearance had somehow changed, just enough to make Him familiar and unfamiliar at the same time. As though I knew Him from somewhere but could not remember from where, but when the man standing before me called me "Woman" and spoke my name, I knew immediately who was speaking to me, and when He smiled at me, I knew why He felt so familiar.[241]

I made my way into His arms and rested my head against His chest, and He cradled me the way He had so many times before. When He attempted to step back, I boldly put my arms around His waist and pressed Him to me tightly, as though I never intended to let Him go ever again. Until He said, "You can't hold me here, Mary. You have to let me go."[242] Stepping back was the hardest thing I have ever had to do, but doing it meant helping Him, so I released Him, and delivered the message He sent through me.

Even though I was the first to see Yeshua after His resurrection, I was not the only one to see Him, and those who also saw Him had the same reaction, without exception. At first sight, no one recognized Him as our Teacher, until He said or did something very familiar to that person, in a way that only the Teacher could or would say or do. Our

---

[241] John 20:11, 14-16.
[242] John 20:17 (11–17).

eyes could see, our hearts burned within us and we knew.[243] Two of the brothers traveled all the way back to Jerusalem to tell about their encounter with a stranger while walking home to Emmaus.

They said that after hours of talking with him along the road, they were led them to a deeper understanding concerning matters important to GOD, and that his way of teaching reminded them of the Rabbi. As the stranger was blessing the meal, the prayer was one they had heard the Teacher pray many times before, and it was then their eyes could see He was their Teacher, and then He left them.

What I have never understood are those disciples who touched and spoke with Yeshua after His resurrection, even worshipped Him, and still doubted it was their Teacher come back from the dead.[244] Leaving me to wonder for the rest of my life whether they ever really knew Him at all.

When Yeshua appeared the final time, all of His disciples we were together in one room.[245] His first words to us were of peace, because fear was evident, and His closing words to us were about faith, our faith in Him in particular. It was much later before I understood why He wondered whether, when He came again, He would find anyone living who still had faith in Him.[246] When He invited anyone to ask a question, many had questions, and He patiently answered them one by one. The last one came from Cephas, "What is the sin of the world?"[247]

---

[243] Acts 13:30. See other acts of resurrection in 1 Kings 17:21-22 (17-24); 2 Kings 4:32-35 (28-37); Psalm 71:20; Mark 5:41-42 (21-43); Luke 7:13-15 (11-17; John 11:40-44 (1-44).
[244] Luke 24:31 (13-33); Matthew 28:17.
[245] John 20:24–26.
[246] Luke 18:8.
[247] Leloup, *The Gospel of Mary Magdalene*, 25.

To this day, I can still remember the look Yeshua gave him before responding.

"There is no sin. It is you who makes sin exist when you act according to the habits of your corrupted nature. *That* is where sin lies. This is why the Good has come into your midst. Good acts together with the elements of your nature to reunite it with its roots. This is why you become sick, and why you die. It is the result of your actions. What you do brings you closer to, or takes you further away, from GOD. Those who have ears let them hear.[248]

"Attachment to matter gives rise to passions against nature, and then trouble arises in the whole body. This is why I tell you to be in harmony. If you are out of balance, take inspiration from the manifestations of your *true* nature. Those who have ears let them hear.

"Be vigilant, and allow no one to mislead you by saying 'Here it is!' or 'There it is!' For it is within *you* that the Son of Man dwells. Go to GOD, for those who seek GOD will find GOD. Walk forth and announce the gospel of the kingdom. Impose no law other than that to which I have witnessed, and do not add more laws to those given in the Torah, lest you become bound by them."[249]

After Yeshua left us, and before each of the disciples began going their own way, there was one final meeting.

---

[248] Ibid.
[249] Leloup, *The Gospel of Mary Magdalene*, 27, 29; Matthew 7:7-11; Luke 11:9-13 (see also Deuteronomy 4:2, 12:32; Matthew 22:37-40, 24:23; Mark12:30-31; Luke 10:25-28, 17:20–21).

## The Question Is

The meeting was to discuss what to do next, because no one knew what next to do. All twenty-four disciples attended—twelve women and twelve men—but no one said a word until one of the brothers spoke the problem aloud.

"How are we supposed to go out into the world and announce this good news about the kingdom and the Child of Humanity? If they didn't hesitate to kill Him, why should they spare us?"[250]

The bickering began almost immediately. A different brother objected to the question because he felt it suggested he might not be brave. A few of the others began arguing as to who among them was the greatest and most capable man, a behavior Yeshua had intensely disliked,[251] and the remainder of the brothers appeared to be in shock, uncertain of what to do or say. As the arguing grew louder, the eleven sisters and I exchanged glances but not words, watching and waiting to see what would happen. Their names, for the record, are Kinneret, Ziv, Dalia, Joanna, Chava, Lior, Yonah, Devorah, Elke, Charna, and Leah.[252]

Early on in His ministry, Yeshua learned not to expect full faith on a large scale. He overcame that limitation by choosing for Himself one female follower for every male follower chosen for Him by GOD.

---

[250] Karen L. King, "The Gospel of Mary," in *The Nag Hammadi Scriptures*, ed. Marvin Myers, (New York: HarperCollins, 2007), 742. "Child of Humanity" is the "Son of Man" listed in Matthew 20:28; Luke 19:10; John 3:13, etc., and "Son of God" is listed in Matthew 14:33; Luke 1:35, etc.
[251] Matthew 18:1; Mark 9:33–34; Luke 9:46, 22:24.
[252] See *The Testimony of Judas*, 50.

That farsighted decision immediately increased twofold the number of His disciples and potential servants for GOD.

While the brothers went out in pairs of two to do ministry, the sisters and I trailed Yeshua as He went from place to place preaching in each of the brother's hometown.[253] During the day, we ministered with Him to those in need, in the evenings, He taught us the ways of His peace. The lesson on the sisters' minds that day in the meeting was of Yeshua saying that quarreling and lack of harmony cannot be overcome using disharmony, or by crossing swords in war, but by actively keeping quiet and still until certain how best to proceed.

I saw Cephas huddle with Andrew before standing to take control of the room. When he raised his hand high above his head, the commotion turned to order almost immediately. He looked around the room, smiling as he said, "Mary, we know the Teacher loved you differently from other women, so tell us what you remember of anything He told you that we have not yet heard."[254] Whether he was asking the question with a sincere heart I cannot say, but I chose to respond as though he was.

"Cephas, what you're asking of me is something that should rightly be asked of everyone here. What did the Teacher tell you when you were alone with Him, or when you, John and James were alone with Him?[255] All of us have spent time alone with the Teacher, and no doubt heard something that has never been shared with the rest of us." Heads in the room nodded in agreement. "But I'll gladly share with the others

---

[253] Matthew 10:5, 11:1; Mark 6:7; Luke 9:1, 10:1–2.
[254] Leloup, *The Gospel of Mary Magdalene*, 31.
[255] Matthew 17:1; Mark 5:37; Luke 9:28.

what I recently shared with you, Cephas, because the words concern us all and were meant for all of us to hear.

"Before the Teacher revealed Himself to some of you after His resurrection, He showed Himself first to me and then sent me to bring you this message. He said, "Go to my brothers and sisters and tell them I am returning to my Father, who is also your Father, to my GOD, who is also your GOD."[256]

I turned to Cephas and said, "You remember how I came and delivered those words to you and the other brothers—words none of you had heard before—and how none of you believed me when I said the words came from our Teacher?

"Brothers and sisters, our Teacher has faithfully completed His work of reuniting us with GOD, the source of our human and spiritual roots, so that it no longer matters that each of us heard something from Him that not everyone else was present to hear. What matters in this moment is remembering the two commands we all heard together, which He gave us to live by as sons and daughters of GOD."[257]

Cephas sat down, and I stood to continue speaking.

"We are to love GOD with all our heart, soul and strength, the commandment Moses received. The Rabbi added the word mind to the teaching because the mind is where our thoughts arise and live, and our lives are shaped by our thoughts, our thoughts are guided by the feelings

---

[256] John 20:17.
[257] John 1:12; Mark 5:34.

and affections we hold in our heart, and those feelings and affections guide our body's behavior and become the habits we keep. This kinship between what we think and do is why we must always take good care to guard how and what we think.[258]

"The other command our Teacher gave us was that we are to love our neighbor, to do for and to them what we would done for and to ourselves, but He expanded our understanding of who our neighbor is. They include not only those who live in the same community as we do, or who are like us by birth, but also those who live outside our borders, beliefs and traditions, and for daring to transform our minds in this way—for daring to teach that GOD's love extends equally to Gentiles— our Teacher was executed.[259]

"The entire Law of GOD was written with these two obligations in mind—love of GOD and love of neighbor—even the ancient prophets relied on them for guidance, as they sought to know and understand what GOD expected and wanted them to do. If we do likewise, if we consider first these two commands, no doubt we will also know what to do and say when we go out into the world to tell others what the Teacher has said.

---

[258] Deuteronomy 6:5; Proverbs 4:23 (20–27); Matthew 6:21, 22:37; Mark 12:30; Luke 10:27, 12:34.
[259] Deuteronomy 4:44, 6:5, Matthew 22:39; Mark 12:31; Luke 10:27. "Gentile" in this sense means non-Jews and anyone others have labeled as different or offensive.

"But obedience to these commands is no guarantee harm won't come to us. The prophet Ezekiel had to run for his life, hunted down like an animal, and Jeremiah wished our loud that he had never been born. The Rabbi told us a student is not greater than the one teaching them—making our brother's question a fair and honest one—why *should* our lives be spared when our Teacher's was not?[260] Some of us will die in the same manner as our Teacher did, some will be arrested and taken to prison, but if our heart's desire is to be counted among the ones who will sit by the Teacher when He ascends to His throne,[261] we must prepare ourselves now, by having fellowship with Him in suffering as well.

"Each of us has a role to play in GOD's plan of salvation, no less so than our Teacher did. By describing Himself as the vine and us as branches meant to bear good fruit, and in announcing it is harvest time but lamenting the shortage of laborers,[262] He was telling us as clearly as He could that He needs our help almost as much as we need His, and as He needed GOD's. If we attempt to rely on ourselves for the strength to do our work, we will be neither strong enough nor capable enough to function as earthen vessels through whom GOD's divine compassion and the fulfillment of GOD's promises come. Relying on anything other than the LORD has always been a risky and delicate way to live, but if fear of death is enough to stop any of us from making ourselves available to GOD, perhaps it is best to walk away now.

"What will make our work even more challenging is that those to whom we are being sent still believe a separation exists between this

---

[260] 1 Kings 19:2–3; Jeremiah 20:1-2, 14-18; Matthew 10:24-25; Luke 6:40; John 15:20.
[261] Mark 10:40.
[262] Matthew 9:37–38; Luke 10:2; John 5:19, 14:10-11, 15:4–5.

world and the next, and this illusion is as real to them as being reunited with GOD is to us. Like us, their mind and heart tell their body what to do, and with all its heart, soul and strength their body does as commanded. The difference between them and us is, they feel free to say and do what they want no matter who gets hurts and GOD's gift of salvation is a threat, rather than a rescue. Equally important is this. If we attempt to approach anyone without first understanding and believing in our own deliverance, we have no new message to preach or good news to share.

"This world is not our home. We are sojourners on the Earth,[263] and each of us must answer for him or herself the question of how best to move forward in faith rather than fear, in service rather than in control, as we hold tightly to the reality of GOD's love and our *true* nature as children of GOD. But knowing and believing these things won't always be enough to keep us feeling balanced, because while there is no sin in us, as our Teacher said, neither have we reached the state of our Father's perfection.[264] Even the strongest among us will become weak from time to time, whenever our imperfections make themselves visible to remind us that we are rooted in GOD. That it is GOD who holds us, and all things, together. Let us not behave fearfully or despairingly, as do those who have no hope, because our LORD and GOD will be with us no matter where we go."[265]

When I said the word go, Cephas motioned to Andrew, who quickly stood and loudly said, "Brothers and sisters, what do you think about the things she has been telling us? I don't believe the Teacher said

---

[263] Psalm 84:1-5, 119:19; John 15:18-19 (see also Philippians 3:20; Hebrews 13:14; 1 Peter 2:11-12).
[264] Matthew 5:48.
[265] Deuteronomy 3:8; Joshua 1: 5,9; Psalm 23:4; Isaiah 43:1-3; Matthew 28:20.

these things to her, because these ideas are too different from those tradition has taught us!" Cephas then rose to his feet and looked around the room. Pointing his finger at me, he said with disbelief, "Are we to believe that the Teacher shared secrets with a woman without our knowing about it—are we now expected to change our customs and listen to *this* woman? Does she really expect us to believe the Teacher chose her over us?"[266]

The room erupted into chaos. Silence returned as I began speaking again.

"My brother Cephas, what on Earth can you be thinking? Do you really believe that what I said is just in my imagination—that I invented this vision? Do you honestly see me as someone who says one thing but means another? Or is it that you believe I would lie about our Teacher?"[267]

Before he could respond, Levi jumped to his feet and said, "Cephas, you have always been an angry person. Now I see you rejecting and dismissing a woman just as our adversaries do, but if the Teacher held Mary up as being worthy, who are you to reject her? He knew her very well. The truth is that He loved her more than us. It would be better, therefore, for us to be ashamed and become fully human like her, so that the Teacher can take root in us as He has in Mary. We should grow as He commanded us, and go forth to spread the good news of the gospel

--------

[266] Leloup, *The Gospel of Mary Magdalene*, 37.
[267] Ibid, 39.

without trying to lay down any rules or laws other than those the Teacher confirmed."[268]

That was the last time all twenty-four of us were together in one room. Ever since that day, I have spent my allotted time trying to live and work in such a way that GOD might choose me to sit at Yeshua's right side, as He now sits at GOD's right hand.[269]

---

[268] Ibid.
[269] Psalm 110:1; Matthew 20:23; Mark 10:40, 16:19; Luke 22:69.

## Great or First?

*(Mary looks down for a few moments before continuing her testimony)*

Levi was correct when he said Cephas was an angry man, but Cephas was also bold and gifted, sometimes recklessly so, and he enjoyed being the center of attention, yet he was also the first among us to publicly confess Yeshua as the promised Messiah send by GOD.[270] The reward for his confession of faith was Yeshua's promise to pass the keys to the kingdom of heaven on to him.[271] I can easily imagine that it is a difficult thing to say no, when being handed the keys controlling access to an empire. Harder still is to remain humble once they are in your hand. The question no one knew the answer to was how Cephas would use the keys. Would he use them, as Yeshua had done, to unlock the gates[272] leading into a new Jerusalem so that all who wanted to could go in, or would he use them to keep certain gates locked and certain people locked out? That was his test,[273] and during his season of testing, Hasatan[274] sifted Cephas like wheat, just as Yeshua said would happen.

The purpose of any kind of sifting is to separate, and Hasatan's plan of attack has always been to separate the Believer from GOD. Cephas' sifting began in earnest the moment he denied knowing his

---

[270] Matthew 16:13–17.
[271] Matthew 16:18-19.
[272] Revelation 21:9-12.
[273] Luke 22:31-32.
[274] Hasatan, the Hebrew word for The Accuser or The Adversary (or Satan). The definite article Ha (or English 'The') indicates the word is a function rather than a proper name.

Teacher—not once, but on three separate occasions.[275] Job endured sifting as well, when his good life was no more.[276] In Cephas' case, fame blinded him.

Many of the faithful began looking to him for spiritual direction and guidance. Hailed a great leader, thousands of people became Believers in response to his preaching, and when he healed a crippled man so that he could walk again, he became known as a great healer.[277]

When I heard later that Cephas had sentenced a husband and wife to death for telling a lie, and that fear was replacing joy in the hearts of Believers,[278] I knew he had lost his way. He was arrested and imprisoned, as many disciples were, but was released when many others were not. Yeshua had prayed on his behalf, as He promised to do.[279]

When Cephas finally passed through his time of testing, he came to himself[280] and regained possession of a right mind and a right spirit, like the other prodigal son.

What happened in Cephas' life is why I have aspired to be first, rather than great.[281]

---

[275] Matthew 26:70, 72, 74; Mark 14:68, 70, 71: Luke 22:31, 57, 58b, 60; John 18:17b, 25c, 27.
[276] Job 1:6-12 (1:1-2:10).
[277] Acts 1:15–17, 2:14–41, 3:1–8, 4:4, 5:13–15.
[278] Acts 5:1-11.
[279] Luke 22:31-32.
[280] Luke 15:17; Acts 12:11.
[281] Matthew 20:25-27; Mark 10:42-45.

## The Long Way Home

Before Yeshua left us, Cephas openly questioned Him about me, and Yeshua rebuked him, saying, "If I want her to live until I come again, what business is that of yours?" Not long after, a rumor saying I would never die began to spread.[282]

The idea was so impossible, I shook my head at anyone who believed it and gave the matter no further thought. Not until everyone I had ever known was dead and buried, and their children after them. When no one who knew me remained alive to recognize me, I vanished into a scandalous invisibility involving demons and prostitutes. Yet, here I sit this many generations later giving this testimony.

How GOD has kept me alive these many years, I do not know. The how is as unknown to me as is the mystery shrouding Yeshua's resurrection. When I inquired of GOD about the long length of my life, the response came back in the form of a question. "Why did Methuselah live to be 969 years of age?" I gave the only answer there was to give— the same answer others before me had given—"Lord, you know,"[283] and then went on living my life.

I have taken the long way home, but at long, last, my own body is growing still, the reason for this final testimony making known what happened. I offer my testimony for the sake of GOD who said, "Turn back, and live!" for the sake of Yeshua who said, "Repent, for the

---

[282] John 21:21-23.
[283] Genesis 5:27; Ezekiel 37:3.

kingdom of heaven is at hand!" and for the sake of the whole world, because of what is still to come.[284]

When GOD sent Jonah to the people of Nineveh to warn them about a coming destruction, Jonah delivered the warning with reproach and disgust, not caring if any of the people lived, but they listened to the warning and changed their ways, so that GOD took pity, and did not bring destruction upon them, causing Jonah to become angry.[285]

Then GOD sent Yeshua to warn people everywhere about the destruction coming on the whole Earth. He delivered the warning not with doom or condemnation but with love, trying to save as many people as possible. Because unlike Jonah, even one saved soul brings Yeshua great joy.[286]

The divine compassion and grace that once withheld destruction from raining down on Nineveh, is the same compassion and grace that has repeatedly delayed and restrained the wrath coming on the world. GOD's will and intent is always to do good, and GOD takes no pleasure in the death of anyone, but John clarified there will be no more delay. Between the pouring out of the sixth and seventh bowls containing GOD's righteous wrath—a period of time that feels like no more than half an hour—it would seem that GOD entertains the idea of postponing the end

---

[284] Ezekiel 33:11; Matthew 3:2, 4:17; Mark 1:15; John 14:3; Revelation 22:7a.
[285] Jonah 1:1–3, 3:1–5, 10, 4:1 (1-4). While Nineveh was a three-day journey from one end to the other, the Bible records Jonah only covering one day's journey before shouting, "Forty days and Nineveh will be destroyed!", and then leaving the city.
[286] Matthew 18:12-14; Luke 11:29-30, 19:10; John 3:16-17; 6:39-40.

once again, using another mystery. Until an order comes from heaven that the mystery is not to be written down, ensuring it would not come to be, and that decision has not changed. There will be no more delay.[287]

Life on Earth was to be lived within a linear perspective of time, another one of GOD's creations, which stretches from the beginning to the end. What some call the Alpha and Omega, and others call the first and last, or the past, present and future rolled into one.[288] What is true for all created things is also true for time—it will cease to exist the moment its purpose is fulfilled—and the illusion of time is that it goes on forever without end, until the moment it runs out, and the illusion is revealed for what it always was.

Outside the boundaries of Earth, time is everlastingness—time is without end—but on what day and at what hour time will take its final breath, not even Yeshua knew. He could only tell us what signs to look for in the heavens and on Earth, saying they would be as visible as a tree putting forth its leaves to tell us that summer is near, and that His return would be as unexpected as a thief coming in the middle of the night, when most people are sleeping.[289] His coming is near now, because many of the signs He said to look for are now visible, and all at the same time.

Access to information is at our fingertips, anyone searching for knowledge can find it. People who appear godly on the outside are

---

[287] Psalm 145:8; Isaiah 48:9; Ezekiel 33:11; Revelation 10:1–7.
[288] Genesis 1:3–5, 14; Isaiah 44:6, 48:12; Revelation 1:8, 17, 21:6a, 22:13.
[289] Matthew 24:3–36, 42–44; Mark 13:1–37; Luke 18:8b, 21:5–36; Revelation 1:7, 3:3, 16:15, 22:12.

leading other people astray. Progress and prosperity have led to people loving pleasure more than GOD. Violence, in all its forms, has flooded all four corners of the Earth. The weight of waiting has caused the burning love many once had for GOD and Yeshua to grow lukewarm, and His call to stay woke is now disturbing and offensive to blind guides who call good evil and evil good, and teach light as darkness and darkness as light.[290]

World leaders and powers speak in grand and hopeful terms about the future of tomorrow, because they cannot see and are unwilling to accept that the coming future is when the not-yet-things of GOD will become as they should and shall be. So deep is their denial, they likely will not see what is coming until it is fully revealed. The Earth is on fire, and the stability and balance GOD put in place on Earth to favor habitation is reverting to chaos, changes that will involve the sun, moon, wind, rain, and the Earth itself.[291] GOD's plan of salvation has spread across the entire Earth, and the beast from the Earth[292] is a known entity. This is some of the evidence signifying just how near the final day and hour are.

The praise of Believers everywhere should be getting louder now as each day passes, because the King of kings, the Lord of lords, the One who saves, is making His way back to collect the keepers of the faith, the ones who believed they could afford to lose everything except

---

[290] Isaiah 5:21, 9:16; Jeremiah 50:6; Ezekiel 13:8-10; Daniel 12:4; Matthew 7:15-16, 15:10-14, 24:42-44; Luke 21:34-36; John 3:19Acts 20:28-30; Romans 13:11-12; 2 Corinthians 11:12-15; Colossians 4:5-6; 1 Thessalonians 5:1-11; 2 Timothy 3: 1-7; Revelation 3:2, 15-16.
[291] Revelation 8:12, 11:19, 16:3-4, 10-12, 18.
[292] Genesis 1:1-2a, 3-19; Matthew 28:19; Mark 16:15; Revelation 13:1-18.

GOD. So, hold tightly to whatever measure of faith you have, because what matters now is not who others decide who and what you and I are, but rather who's going to glory. When our Lord appears, there will be no place anyone can run to and hide, but down to the very last minute of time, GOD's forgiveness and pardon remain present and available for the asking, because GOD's character and willful intent is always to do good to others.

If you seek GOD with your whole heart, you will find GOD, and if your heart can still be broken, there is still hope. Even right now is not too late to decide for GOD, who does not will that anyone should perish.[293]

This declaration is to the Christian church:

Your offense in the sight of GOD is grounded in your effort to do what Yeshua said was impossible to do, to serve GOD and wealth, the most attractive and enslaving of all the opiates the world has to offer. Your one purpose was to go out into the world, without becoming part of its illusions,[294] and use the power and authority you received from the LORD[295] to conquer the marketplace, free those taken hostage by life's temptations and circumstances, and create a more just and level playing field for the poor. Instead, the market cornered you, brought you to your knees and left you wringing your hands over insufficient budgets, while

---

[293] 2 Chronicles 15:2; Proverbs 8:17; Jeremiah 29:12–14; Joel 2:32.
[294] John 17:14.
[295] Matthew 10:1; Mark 6:7; Luke 9:1.

you went on pretending you were wealthy, prosperous and in need of nothing.[296]

It is no small matter that the final mention of the church in the Good Book is neither good news nor a favorable report. Even as I speak, heaven is waiting to see whether the church will follow the divine recommendation to use its financial dividends to purchase eye cream and righteousness, so that it can see and have a place in the new Jerusalem.[297]

GOD has patiently allowed this day, the next day, the day after that, and on and on without exception. Stretching out the illusion of time that a sunrise will forever follow a sunset, but there will now be no more delay.

This declaration is to Jerusalem:

Your offense in GOD's sight is rooted in your lack of grace, your refusal to extend to others the hospitality and kindness you yourselves received, and your appetite for persecuting and prosecuting anyone who dares to oppose or contest your self-appointed sovereignty. To you, a heartbroken GOD declares in the latter days the words spoken to you nearer to the beginning of days:

"Your origin and birth originated in the land of the Canaanites. Your father was an Amorite and your mother a Hittite. As for your birth, on the day you were born your cord was not cut, no one washed you with water to clean you or rubbed you with salt, or wrapped you in swaddling clothes. No eye pitied you enough to do any of these things to you, not

---

[296] Revelation 3:17.
[297] Revelation 2:5b, 3:18.

even out of compassion. Instead, on the day you were born, they put you and your mother out alone in an open field to die. Every eye that looked on you saw the two of you as an abomination because you offended them, but when I passed by and saw you wallowing in your own blood, I said to you in your blood, 'Live!' A second time I said to you, 'Live!' and then made you flourish like a plant in the field. When I passed by you again and saw you, you were at the age for love, and I spread the corner of my garment over you to cover your nakedness. I made a vow to you, entered into a covenant with you, and you became mine. I remembered my covenant with you in the days of your youth, and I established for you an everlasting covenant as promised, but you despised the oath by breaking the covenant. Therefore, I shall deal with you as you have done."[298]

Two questions remain unanswered, Jerusalem. Are you able to thrive, and can anyone break GOD's covenant and escape the consequences?

Both the Christian church and Jerusalem have a mission that neither can complete alone, both stand in need of deliverance and neither has righteous standing from which to rebuke or throw stones at the other. Leaving only the goodness, mercy and grace of GOD on which to depend.

I am Mary of Magdala, the disciple who bears witness to these things. Time does not permit me to tell everything that happened, and if it was available, I cannot be certain the world has enough space to hold all the words.[299]

---

[298] Ezekiel 16:3–7a, 17:18–19.
[299] John 21:24–25.

May GOD's steadfast love comfort you, may GOD's mercy come to you that you may live. May your heart be blameless so that you may not be put to shame, and may GOD's love and protection be with you until time is no more.[300]

---

[300] Adapted from Psalm 119:77-80.

Bibliography

Alter, Robert. *The Hebrew Bible: A Translation with Commentary*, Vol. 1. New York: W.W. Norton & Company, 2019.

Balz, Horst, and Gerhard Schneider, eds. *Exegetical Dictionary of the New Testament*, Vols. 2 & 3. Grand Rapids: Eerdmans, 1991, 1993.

Baillie, John, John T. McNeil, and Henry P. Van Dusen, eds. *Calvin: Institutes of the Christian Religion*. Vol. 1. Philadelphia: Westminster Press, 1960.

Buchanan, George W. "The Priestly Teacher of Righteousness." *Revue De Qumran* 6, no. 4 (24) (1969): 553–558.

Burse, Cynthia F. *A Little Bible Dictionary*. Self-published for private use, 2022.

De Boer, Esther A. "Mary Magdalene and the Disciple Jesus Loved," http://www.lectio.unibe.com, 1/2000, ISSN 1661-3317.

Foundation for Inner Peace. *A Course in Miracles*. Mill Valley, CA: Foundation for Inner Peace, 1992.

Ghose, Tia. "Animal Sacrifice at Temple Powered Ancient Jerusalem's Economy." NBC News, September 4, 2013, https://www.nbcnews.com/sciencemain/animal-sacrifice-temple-powered-ancient-jerusalems-economy-8C11073738.

Jews for Jesus. "The Role of Women in the Bible," https://jewsforjesus.org/learn/the-role-of-women-in-the-bible, accessed June 24, 2024.

Justino, Ramon K. "Mary Magdalene: Author of the Fourth Gospel?" https://southerncrossreview.org/37/jusino.htm, accessed June 24, 2024.

Kalas, J. Ellsworth. *The Thirteen Apostles*. Nashville: Abingdon Press, 2002.

King, Karen L. "The Gospel of Mary," in *The Nag Hammadi
   Scripture: The Revised and Updated Translation of Sacred
   Gnostic Texts*. ed. Marvin Meyer. New York: HarperCollins:
   2007.

Macinnis, Adam. "Study: Trauma-Informed Bible Reading
   Reduces Depression, Anxiety and Anger." Christianity Today,
   May 3, 2021,
   https://www.christianitytoday.com/news/2021/may/bible-
   reading-study-trauma-ptsd-covid19-mental-health.html.

Meyer, Marvin, ed. *The Nag Hammadi Scriptures: The
   Revised and Updated Translation of Sacred Gnostic Texts*. New
   York: HarperCollins, 2007.

Pagels, Elaine. *The Gnostic Gospel*. New York: Vintage
   Books, 1979.

Telushkin, Rabbi Joseph. *The Book of Jewish Values: A Day-
   by-Day Guide to Ethical Living*. New York: Bell Tower, 2000.

Van Oort Johannes. "Irenaeus's Knowledge of the Gospel of
   Judas: Real or False? An Analysis of the Evidence in Context."
   *HTS Teologiese Studies/Theological Studies* 69, no. 1 (May 6,
   2013), http://dx.doi.org/10.4102/hts.v69i1.1916.

Whiston, William, trans. *Josephus, The Complete Works*.
   Nashville: Thomas Nelson Publishers, 1998.

www.ingramcontent.com/pod-product-compliance
Lightning Source LLC
Chambersburg PA
CBHW021153130626
46554CB00005B/1798